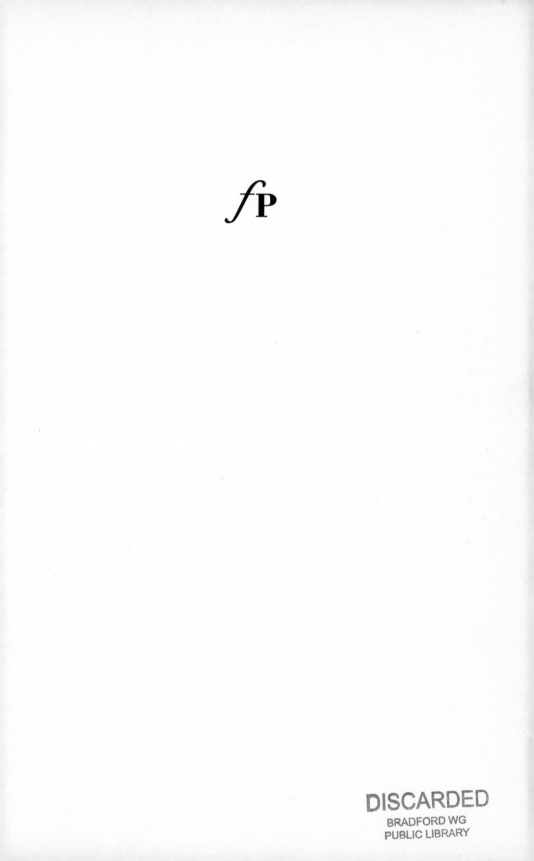

f**P**

lighten

Love What You Have,
Have What You Need,
Be Happier With Less

up

Peter Walsh

FREE PRESS

New York   London   Toronto   Sydney

*f*P
Free Press
A Division of Simon & Schuster, Inc.
1230 Avenue of the Americas
New York, NY 10020

First Free Press hardcover edition January 2011
FREE PRESS and colophon are trademarks of Simon & Schuster, Inc.

For information about special discounts for bulk purchases,
please contact Simon & Schuster Special Sales at 1-866-506-1949
or business@simonandschuster.com

The Simon & Schuster Speakers Bureau can bring authors
to your live event. For more information or to book an event
contact the Simon & Schuster Speakers Bureau at 1-866-248-3049
or visit our website at www.simonspeakers.com.

Designed by Katy Riegel

Manufactured in the United States of America

10 9 8 7 6 5 4 3 2 1

Library of Congress Cataloging-in-Publication Data

Walsh, Peter.
    Lighten up : love what you have, have what you need, be happier with
less / Peter Walsh.
       p. cm.
    1. Finance, Personal.   2. Happiness.   3. Orderliness.   I. Title.
    HG179.W3164 2011
    332.024—dc22   2010030244

ISBN 978-1-4391-5514-1
ISBN 978-1-4391-6008-4 (ebook)

To
Carol Greenblatt
1941–2010

contents

We tend to forget that happiness doesn't come as a result of getting something we don't have, but rather of recognizing and appreciating what we do have. —FREDERICK KOENIG

Nothing can bring you happiness but yourself.
—RALPH WALDO EMERSON

lighten up

Measuring Happiness—How a Life with Less Can Be a Life with More

PERHAPS YOU'RE READING THIS while browsing in a bookstore. If so, glance over at the woman across the way when she's not looking, the one scanning titles of books on a table and searching for her next engrossing read. She's well dressed, appears healthy and happy, and looks intelligent and strong willed, someone who could be a friend or neighbor. You can't picture this woman as someone who feels extraordinarily lost and as emotionally bankrupt as her bank account. She is estranged from her husband and friends, disconnected from her children, stifled by debt, angry and resentful at how much her life has changed in recent years, and terrified that she'll never get back to that place where money was abundant and she felt so in control of her life. But if you were to follow her home and get to know this woman, you'd find that her looks defy everything about her. She doesn't know who she is anymore, and in fact can't find her way "home."

She's got mail dating back three months that she hasn't opened for fear of another past-due notice. Her teenage children have no idea that their college funds have been squandered and there's no money for summer camp this year. Ever since her husband lost his job a year ago and money got excruciatingly tight, their relationship hasn't been the same. They can't afford to get a divorce, though the thought has crossed her mind. She harbors a grudge toward her husband for telling her that she's got to learn to live on less, and that their previous lifestyle is gone. Conversations about money erupt into ferocious fighting, and the thought of accepting this new reality is terrifying for both of them. How can she be happy? Where will she get the courage to find joy and peace of mind in all this mess? **Who is she now?** What pains her the most is that things fell apart so quickly. Just a few years ago, life was good and filled with opportunities. They always had money in the bank, plans for another vacation, and a clean and tidy house that their friends envied. Then came the Great Recession. Overnight, all bets were off.

Now the fear of losing their home looms large. They have burned through their savings and much of their retirement money. The woman does whatever she can to soothe her overwhelming anxiety, trying to find pleasure in boutiques and clothing stores—anything to put a damper on her emotional pain and deepening depression. She can't stop shopping. She pawned some of her jewelry last week just to pay for basic living expenses this month and find more money for shopping. When she pulls out a credit card to make a small purchase for herself, she feels guilty on the one hand, and on the other, wonders when someone will come bail her out like the government did for Wall Street. Somehow she gets through each day by pushing the reality of her situation to the back of her mind. If she just doesn't think about it too much she can manage it.

This woman is not unlike millions who are struggling to make ends meet through tough financial times while at the same time trying to preserve their emotional well-being. She may even be like you. And you are like everyone else.

I don't need to remind you what's been going on in America since I last wrote a book. Treading water has become second nature as we attempt to recover from the worse financial fallout since the

Great Depression. Technically, the most recent recession may have been declared over already, but that doesn't negate the fact so many of us are still stuck in its debris. Millions of people remain lost, disheartened, uninspired, debt-ridden, and frustrated by having to live on less. Some of us are paying the price of living deep in an orgy of consumption for the past decade—surviving giddily off of borrowed money and a kind of pay-as-you-go happiness. But others of us have just been bystander victims of the financial tsunami that has swept through the country. The combination of an unexpected job loss, medical crisis, and tumbling net worth due to the real estate decline, for example, can be enough to devastate even the strongest and savviest of financial planners. And this kind of financial change can steal not only your happiness, but also your sense of self.

Regardless of your unique story and experience these past couple of years, what's obvious, now, is that the time of personal reckoning has come: we need to change the way we think about our finances, our lives, and what brings us happiness and fulfillment. It's time to seriously clear out the psychological clutter tied to money and finances and the hurdles to happier lives that are running, railroading, or ruining our lives.

You can either continue living in denial or (and my guess is you're considering alternatives because you're reading this book) you can learn how to navigate this current tsunami that has affected all our lives and create a new path of hope, happiness, and well-being for you and your family. The old adage rings true and begs to be repeated: *With crisis comes great opportunity.* I honestly believe this and think that if we wallow in our collective problems and fail to see the chance for something great here, then we're seriously missing the point! That said, you must be brave enough to seize the opportunity. If you'll come along, together we can use that to our advantage.

Glance again at that lady standing nearby and now pretend that she turns to you and wonders what it's like to live *your* life. Your story might not be so extreme, but how much of what she sees on the outside contradicts what's hammering you on the inside? Do you look strong but confront an inner turmoil daily about how to rebalance your life now that things aren't what they used to be? Do fears about the future and of "not having enough" keep you up at night? Are you physically tough but mentally weak and drained from relentless thoughts about your financial situation—and the fact that you're struggling to define yourself and your life in a way that makes sense anymore? We all measure our happiness in different ways. Many of the people I work with find it hard to distinguish happiness from getting more stuff. For these people, better is measured by more and their possessions have become the measure of their well-being. Chasing more and having more has come to mean that I'll somehow *be* more; that if I just buy the right things I can somehow acquire the life I want and will then—of course—be happy. It's a common theory. And a great recipe for disaster!

It almost always takes a crisis for people to make big changes in their lives. I hear from families all the time that their loved ones—parents, spouse, friends—are wrecking their lives with clutter, that it just can't go on like this anymore. The stuff they own has damaged the happiness they want. Well, we've reached the same kind of crisis with money. Even though it may fly in the face of what we've been conditioned to believe, owning more or the pursuit of more simply is *not* better, for ourselves, our families, our communities, or our planet. Worse still, the "more" that we chase might just be the single biggest reason that happiness escapes us. We need to reframe our attitudes toward our stuff and our happiness. We need to rethink how we spend money and what's truly important if we want to improve the quality of our lives and the future of our families.

This very well may be the most important book I've written. Unlike my previous works, from *It's All Too Much: An Easy Plan for Living a Richer Life with Less Stuff,* which focused on physical clutter, to *Enough Already!: Clear the Emotional and Mental Clutter to Create the Life You Want,* which dealt with damaging mental and emotional clutter, this book comes at a time when people need to hear a clear and unambiguous message the most. It comes when tens of millions are wrestling with serious financial problems that invade every aspect of their lives, and no matter how hard they try to change directions and find solutions, they continue to hit walls, go in reverse, or just give up entirely. It also comes at a time when record numbers report their dissatisfaction with their relationships, frustration with their job, and an overwhelming sense of unhappiness with life itself. And—like clutter—the pile of misfortune, exasperation, deferred dreams, and troubled relationships keeps accumulating. Some of you may have decluttered in the past, performed some serious spring cleaning, and invested good intentions in your attempts to organize your life. But was it all to no avail when the recession hit? Did the physical stuff get cleared out but leave a huge emotional and personal vacuum in its place? What happened? Where did you go wrong? Why couldn't those good intentions help you to avoid, at least a little bit, the ravages of the recession? The answers to those questions are in this book. And so are the straightforward solutions for turning this around for good. Some say that money is the root of all evil. I'm not a subscriber to that theory, but I do believe that our attitude to things, and especially our attitude to money, has hugely contributed to the mess we're in.

The news isn't all bad. I know that thousands, if not millions, of families are taking advantage of the downturn to reboot their values and their plans for their futures. This is a huge plus. We've lost money but we've found a sense of priority in our lives. We are more aware of the difference between needs versus wants and entitlements. We are increasingly conscious of our environment, and no longer have to drive the heftiest SUV on the road. We don't care for another 2,000 square feet of living space if we can live comfortably with what we have and pay our mortgage on time. We are more apt (more out of necessity than anything else) to tell our children that they won't be getting x, y, or z these holidays. And I sense that there is a growing awareness that less really can be more. That being thrifty, when done right, can be surprisingly liberating, pleasurable, and rewarding all the way down to our happiness centers. When

I ask people which words describe how they want to live now, I don't hear words like "big" and "large"; I hear the words "simply," "peacefully," "modestly," "with less stress," and "with more real connection to loved ones." Happiness doesn't come with a hugely expensive price tag, a maxed-out credit card, a crushing mortgage, or keeping up with five thousand "friends" on Facebook! I'm going to show you how thrift allows you to evaluate the world anew. Frugality is not about deprivation at all. Much to the contrary, it's about examining life's possibilities, then homing in on the ones that make you happiest.

That said, our good intentions and renewed values can be undone easily by our ingrained habits and past decisions. Many of us may *want* to live on less but don't know how, having grown so accustomed to the pre-Recession world, and having attached our whole identities to what we own. We still cling to who we were or how much we had to spend before facing (or ignoring) today's realities, and we can't stop equating being happy with having more. We may secretly fight to keep up appearances while continuing to delude ourselves and let our relationships with loved ones erode because we can't talk to them about money and limitations. So how do we rectify this? How do we heal the great divide in our families and come together as a team to fulfill each other's dreams no matter what the economy throws at us? If you're feeling paralyzed by fear, overwhelmed by your money woes, and paying (figuratively, emotionally, and literally) for your past mistakes, how do you move forward and embrace this new world while you're still carrying all the baggage from the old world? Put simply, **How do you live a life of abundance *on less*?** What does that mean? How is this possible—without pretending or feeling that you're being forced to against your will? Can you reclaim a financial life—and be happy—with significantly less?

You know what I'm going to say to that: Yes! Remember what I've always said: it's not about the stuff. Experience has shown again and again that if you focus on "the stuff," you are never going to get to the root cause of a cluttered, unhappy life. I say the same thing about the stuff of money and your financial compass: If you just look at the money (and the credit cards, and interest rates, and rules to retirements accounts, and budgeting formulas, and so on), you will never get at the root of financial distress. If you define yourself by your possessions and financial status, you'll never find peace of mind, lasting contentment, and deep-rooted happiness. You can make spreadsheets, concoct elaborate budgets and spending plans, read the latest personal finance guru's book, or speak with financial advisors until the cows come home. But to truly understand what is happening you have to look at why buying more and acquiring more is so important to you. You have to look at where you're attempting to find happiness and decide whether it's really causing you pleasure or just more pain. It's easy enough to understand the need for change, it's tough to embrace that change in your everyday life. Only then can you get to the heart of your consumption, deal with it in an honest way, and create a vision for the life you want for yourself and your family. Only then can you **define who you really are** and live up to that person every single day with excitement and pleasure.

And that's exactly what we're going to do together in this book. In the same way that I conquered clutter in your home (and on your butt and in your mind) in my previous books, *Lighten Up* will help you to wade through your financial mess, and clear a path to financial health and emotional harmony. I can't guarantee you instant happiness but I am going to show you how to live a life of abundance on less in a way that doesn't plunge you deeper into misery and despair, and my suspicion is that with a changed mind-set will come a sense of calm, authentic personal identity, and . . . yes . . . happiness. Your well-being doesn't have to be measured by monetary wealth. I'll show you how to *capitalize* on where you derive happiness, and help you to realize that your truest sources of pleasure and joy are actually free. I'm also going to help you see that what you already have is more than most people in previous generations ever dreamed about having, and with a little bit of mental and, in some cases, physical rearranging and reprioritizing, you can come to view your life from a completely different place. To that end, I'll show you how to psychologically transform your pain, anxieties, and anguish into a spring of courage and action no matter how much you've lost or had to give up.

If you know anything about me, you know that I tend to think a little differently than most. This book is no different. Most books that offer traditional financial advice and get-out-of-debt programs are a little like diet books. Everyone buys one, everyone reads one, pretty much no one has anything to show for them. Just like fad diets, their lessons are quickly forgotten. The problem is these books often shove the how-to at you without exploring the *whys* underlying your financial distress. It's like the first week of the New Year. We've all been there! You intend to exercise more, to eat better, and to get organized. All goes well for a few days until you hit the first hurdle: a late dinner with friends and one or two drinks more than you intended. The next morning you're too tired to get out of bed to exercise. Suddenly all those resolutions go south! We've all been there—probably many times. Without a realistic plan, a clear understanding of what's likely to trip you up and—most important— an honest assessment of why you want to make these changes in your life, change is unlikely. I want to teach you a lifestyle tuned to the optimal way to live within your means that will keep your life clutter free (and I mean that on every level of the word "clutter"— emotional, physical, financial, and spiritual).

Taking baby steps toward change will slowly alter how you feel, how your financial life looks, and how well you really are. In Part I, we'll explore what kind of life you imagine for yourself and where you *think* you derive your happiness. I'll challenge you to create a realistic vision for your life, reassess what the words "abundance," "needs," "wants," and "entitlements" mean to you, and help you to sketch out a mental blueprint for living out your newfound vision each and every day. Part II will help you use three personal audits to gather information about your situation to instigate changes. This won't necessarily be easy. I'll ask you to face not just the physical stuff and concrete dollar signs, but I'll also ask you to excavate your emotions and address those psychological underpinnings to your habits and attitudes. You'll be challenged to confront your family members, establish tough boundaries under the limits of your family's means, engage the participation of your children even if they are young, and become fully attuned to your own shortfalls and weakness, including the excuses you tell yourself every day just to "get by."

"Just getting by" doesn't work anymore and you know it. It's time to get clear, get real, and get going. Sounds scary? Good! Exciting? Even better! I'll be arming you with all the tools you need to do this, including scripts to use with your partner and kids, specific To-Dos that you can put into practice immediately, exercises for helping you to learn the ropes to living a life of abundance on less, and practical information to create a real, achievable, and personal plan of action. Part III will then give you a checkup and maintenance plan for staying on track with the vision you have for yourself in the real world.

Like I said, this won't be a walk in the park. You'll no doubt find yourself having tough conversations with yourself along the way, as well as difficult discussions with other people in your life, notably the ones who share the same space and contribute to your well-being every day. I've never asked you in the past to sit a five-year-old down and tell him about your debt and what it means to him, or to enforce family meetings with a specific agenda that will stir debate and probably some seriously uncomfortable moments. I've also never asked you to take a personal audit and make the connection between the tension in your life and your everyday habits that aggravate that tension. Until now.

Take a deep breath. For everything you uncover about yourself and your family in this book there will be a clear solution that we craft together so you know what to do. I understand that living on less seems (and feels) unappealing and unnerving, but I'm going to help you change that so it becomes a source of immense power and enjoyment. Keep in mind that the lessons you learn and pass onto your children as you enlist their participation may be the most instrumental and life-enhancing lessons you give them as they mature into thoughtful, productive, money-savvy adults. By the end of this book, you'll have shifted the way you and your family measure happiness, you'll have redefined who you really are and created space for what really matters in your life, and you'll have moved a lot closer to the vision you have for your life than you ever thought possible.

It never ceases to amaze me how, by formulating a clear plan and embracing realistic change, my clients have watched their financial—and other—problems diminish and, in some cases, completely vanish. Among the hundreds of thankful letters that I receive routinely from people who've taken my ideas to heart, there is a singular thought spoken many different ways: "This process has changed my life: I feel empowered and liberated from constant struggle. I'm enjoying the best relationships with my loved ones like never before." They not only share how their financial problems have cleared up since they started following my program, but their overall well-being—both physical and mental—has changed significantly for the better. Significantly.

Mark today as the beginning of a new life. A new sense of honesty with yourself and your world. Accept your past failures and let them inform this new life with resolve. I don't know anyone who hasn't felt jarred by the events over the last several years. The economic storm has ravaged through every demographic and every level of income. We may harbor ill feelings toward our financial institutions and government leaders, but at the end of the day, the change—the recovery—happens at home with you. What I want from everyone who reads this book is to find a greater sense of purpose and power to effect that change on an individual basis. It's within all of us. And yes, that peace, stability, security, and happiness is within you.

part one

From Living on Less to Living with More

1

The Life You Imagine
for Yourself

WHAT WOULD YOU SAY if I asked you what it means to have your life in perfect order? Maybe it's being less stressed about work and money, and having more quality time to spend with family and friends. Maybe it's feeling in total control of your life, your future, and your financial well-being. Maybe it's seeing debt go away so you can plan for bigger dreams and goals. Maybe it's achieving a healthier, more confident version of yourself who is energetic, free from constant worry, and able to accomplish more throughout the day. And maybe it's all of these things plus more.

Chances are you have picked up this book because a voice inside you is saying it's time to make a change. Perhaps you've seen the work I do helping people declutter and organize every aspect of their lives. Maybe you've come to a point in your life where you realize that some serious action is needed to push you in a new direction. Some of you reading this may have tried to declutter your life in the past but became overwhelmed all over again especially once the Great Recession hit. You're still reeling from its consequences, and don't know how to dig yourself out. Or maybe for you it's not the physical clutter that's the problem; it's the emotional and psychological clutter that has accumulated because of changed circumstances. You may be saying something along the following lines:

The recession is supposedly "over" but I feel I'll be living in its wake forever.

My life is an organizational, financial, and emotional nightmare.

I'll never get out from under my debt. And the thought of not having enough petrifies me.

I feel stuck, and unable to change anything for the better in my life.

I am lost. I've lost money, but I've also lost myself. I don't feel in control of my life the way I used to.

Money bought me happiness in the past, and without it I can't find that happiness again.

I thought all the things I've collected and accomplished over the years would have gotten me somewhere, but it's like I've gone in reverse.

I don't know who I am anymore!

Clutter of all kinds is ruining my life, my financial stability, my relationships, and even my sanity.

In other words, *I'm not where I want to be! I'm not who I want to be!*

And you probably don't know where to begin either. "Peace," "harmony," and "happiness" are not words in your daily vocabulary, but you'd give anything for them to be.

THE UPS AND DOWNS

Think for a moment about where you live—your home. There's one truth I will repeat over and over again until it becomes your truth as well; you only have the space you have—you can only fit so much into your home. Your physical space is limited, and so is your money. If you're like most people in the United States today, that amount of space and money has been squeezed considerably thanks to the economic earthquakes that have struck. You may also have noticed that your mental space has been squeezed, too. You only have so much room in your psyche to handle all the disappointments and frustrations you've experienced in recent times. And if you've defined yourself in the past by what you've bought and spent and now you're struggling to figure out who you are in the recession's aftermath, then you know exactly what I mean by feeling lost and out of control on a level that's terrifyingly raw.

Without warning, circumstances changed for all of us—individually and collectively. Whether it's at home or at work, all of us have been asked to do more with less. To live better on less (and with less), and be happy with that. We're being pressured every day to meet the same or more demands with fewer resources. It's amazing how much perception can affect our view of things, too. Even people who haven't lost their jobs or been forced to rethink their spending habits have been psychologically affected by just hearing all the bad news out there. Every day we learn about a new statistic or fact pointing to unwanted outcomes. The uncertainties of the stock market. The rise in depression. The stagnation in the real estate market. The surge in unemployment. It's a bumpy road we're being forced to travel.

Shouldering the weight of all these realities compels us to take stock of our lives and evaluate where we are relative to where we want to be. Haven't you thought more about your happiness or unhappiness in these past couple of years? Haven't you wondered what you could be doing differently to get the results you want out of life? Isn't there a part of you that looks at your surroundings from a purely objective standpoint and asks: *Is this it? Is this as good as it gets?* If there's one thing beneficial about tough times, it's that they have a way of inspiring us in fresh ways. They can corral our innermost wishes and dreams and motivate us to find a way—no matter what—to instigate change even though it may not necessarily be enjoyable at first. Tough times can also serve to point out the times we faked our attempts to "change" in the past, and reset our good intentions with authentic resolve.

If you're familiar with my work then you know that I firmly believe that making any transformation in your life can begin by simply clearing out physical clutter. That's right: you don't have to go much further than just your material possessions to begin a journey that will bring you closer to whatever goals you want—less stress, a lighter load mentally and physically, lower debt, restful sleep at night, a more promising future, healthier relationships, a simpler life. Think of decluttering as your access pass to the life you want, and that's doable given the resources, time, and energy you have. I've done it. I've seen it. I know it's true!

But now it's time to take the decluttering movement to a whole new level. Creating physical space may not be enough for you, especially if you've done the clearing out and are still left feeling at a total loss. You know in your heart that the word "abundance" has nothing to do with possessions but you can't bring yourself to feel like you're living a life of abundance on less. You don't know how to find happiness when happiness used to come wrapped in boxes. Convincing yourself that money doesn't buy happiness is hard to do in the real world. You got used to money buying that rush you called happiness, and I'm here to help you change that.

I'm going to show you how to find an abundant source of happiness that resides far from your financial resources. This book is not just about debt, or getting out of debt for that matter. It's about living a life accepting that what you want is what you likely already have, and that there are very few things that you really need to be content. I'm going to show you step by step how to rearrange your priorities and adjust your attitude so that you can deal with whatever stands between you and the life you want to live.

The Stuff that Dreams Are *Not* Made Of

So we already know the time has come to reevaluate how we live, how we spend, how we collect things, how we pay for goods, how we organize our lives, and how our emotional compass can be swayed by our ideas about money. Now we just have to follow through and take a proper course of action. But even that can be scary. Change is tough—and terrifying! You really do want to get your life in order and adopt a lifestyle that keeps it in good working order, but you wonder how hard it will be. Making lifestyle changes, even little ones, can seem overwhelming at first. You ask: How can I avoid my usual habits? Will I feel deprived or frustrated? Is this program doable given the time I have and the commitments I already have made? Will this just be another exercise in failure for me? What's realistic? What if I don't know how to live on less! What if I've always gotten my happiness from my things and my lifestyle? How do I now change *that* and expect to be happy in the future?

Keep reading, because this book will answer all of these questions and many more. It is easy to get caught up in the idea that having more means being happy—that if we just buy the right things we can somehow acquire the life we want. Success means more stuff. More stuff equals happiness. It's presented as a simple enough equation and seldom questioned. However, I see a very different story every day in my work: homes full of stuff and lives and relationships buckling under the constant duress of financial, professional, and personal demands.

I'm not opposed to surrounding yourself with things that reflect the life you want. Owning is not a bad thing. The problems start when the stuff you own begins to own you. For many of the people I work with it's less about the quality of their lives and relationships and more about the quantity of stuff they can amass. For this reason, I am a firm believer in the power of living clutter free, not just when it comes to the physical stuff, but particularly when it comes to money issues.

As odd as this may sound, my work in helping people declutter their homes and their lives is not so much about "the stuff" as it is about reversing the crippling effect that clutter has in their lives. When we talk of clutter "suffocating" us or feeling "buried" in what we own, the symbolism of those words is huge. Clutter robs us of the life we could be living—not just physically but also socially, emotionally, in our relationships, financially, and spiritually. When we invest most of our energy into acquiring more, something has to suffer—and it always does!

SPECIAL NOTE: *The letters that appear throughout this book are a sampling of the many emails and notes that I receive every day. I've removed names and identifying details, but the sentiments are genuine and the people who have expressed them are real. In addition, the anecdotes in the book about various people are used to illustrate common problems I've encountered in my life and work, but they do not include real names or identifying details and are, in some instances, composites.*

Dear Peter:

Back in July I was downsized from my job. It was a shock to the system. After a while I found that I started lacking more than just money. It was a sense of purpose each day that I missed and each day I felt more and more detached from everyone else. Inspiration was found in a strange kind of way by working for and supporting the food pantry in our small community. So even though we did without a lot of presents this Christmas and scraped together money to pay the bills, we found something instead. We found a sense of priority in our lives. As a family we now know that what seemed necessary before are only material items now. We now know that other people have it far worse than we do and it is within our power to do whatever we can to help the cause. I think as the "Great Recession" continues, people need to figure out not only what they can do without, but what is important in their lives and where their values are. I know we found a better sense of ours and that might not ever have happened if we didn't have to go without.

Toughen Up and Take Ownership of Your Life

I'm not promising that this will be easy or instantaneous, but I do promise that if you commit to decluttering and organizing your finances and your home, the effects will be dramatic for you and your family. The good news is that change is possible but only if you pledge to accept responsibility for your life and decisions, to take action and follow through.

This all starts with you. Unless you choose to own your life, to be responsible for your actions and lapses, there can be no success. Only you can make the changes needed, but I will stand with you every step of the way. These step-by-step processes offer the right balance of structure and adaptability to honor your personal preferences and power of choice. If you do this work honestly, you'll find the experience of going chapter by chapter, and emotional hurdle by emotional hurdle to be liberating. Own your life. Stop blaming others. Commit to your future. Free yourself from the clutches of clutter that continue to disrupt every aspect of your life.

Trust me, this will work. Take a deep breath, relax, and try to evict those negative thoughts that keep bringing you down and stalling you. Be patient with yourself as you begin this journey. Forget about past failures. Focus right now on today, tomorrow, and the ordered life that awaits you in the near future.

POP QUIZ: IS THIS YOU?

How cluttered is your life? Take this quiz to find out. Be honest!

1. How does the topic of money make you feel?
   a. *Empowered; I know money is a source of education and freedom and I'm pretty good with my money. I know where it goes and the exact amount of my debt.*

b. *Indifferent; I'm pretty much in denial about my money problems and try not to think about them too much. Not really sure how much I owe, either.*

c. *Terrified; I know how much I owe and I know I can't ever pay it back. Money is always on my mind and is the reason I'm constantly anxious and have trouble sleeping.*

2. If you had to evacuate your home right now:

   a. *I'd be ready to go in seconds because I can immediately locate all the essential paperwork and valuable items I'd need.*

   b. *I'd need a few hours to get organized. Where are our insurance policies again?*

   c. *I'd panic; I haven't a clue where my important documents are and what I should take or leave behind. Is this really an emergency?*

3. Family friends have invited your family to join them for a long holiday weekend at a beachside resort. You:

   a. *Decline with thanks; it won't fit into your budget this month.*

   b. *Think about it, but when you share the idea with your kids, they beg you to say yes, and you eventually do even though you worry about the related cost in the back of your mind.*

   c. *Accept immediately; how could you let your friends down? It's nice to feel wanted and included.*

4. If you gathered your family around the dining room table tonight and asked each person to share his or her vision for the future (e.g., material possessions, educational or career pursuits, personal goals):

    a. Your family will look at you like you're crazy. They wouldn't understand the purpose of the exercise. They think it's stupid.

    b. Your family will participate but there won't be a meeting of the minds. They think this is a way you are trying to control them. And no one has the same set of priorities.

    c. Your family will confirm things you already know. There's a continual open conversation about money, budgets, goals, priorities, and big-picture planning in the family.

5. When you think of your home and your current lifestyle:

    a. It's a source of stress and anxiety; I don't know how much longer I can keep up with paying overdue bills and hiding the extent of our debt from others. Oh, and don't ask me to host a party anytime soon; it would take me a year to clean up.

    b. I'm hit or miss; I have my weak spots and once or twice a year after everything has built up, I try to attack it and get my life in order again.

    c. I'm very content; I have a good system for staying organized, paying bills, filing paperwork, etc. My home is a reflection of this all year round, too.

6. When I think about the future:

    a. A sense of dread washes over me. I don't know how I'll pay for future expenses and I know my kids will suffer.

    b. Future? I don't think about it. I live day to day. Carpe diem.

    c. I'm prepared and excited. I've planned it that way!

7. The last time I felt happy was:

    a. Today; I love my life!

    b. Before the recession hit.

    c. A long time ago, before I had kids, a mortgage, and too many commitments. Back then, life was simple and the future held so many possibilities!

8. Answer the following questions with a yes or no:

    a. If you lost your job today, could you survive at least three to six months using your savings? (And if you already have lost your job, are you doing okay using savings?)

    b. Do other people (friends, co-workers, partner, kids, pressuring salespeople) make you spend more than you want?

    c. Do you ever shop to make yourself feel better?

    d. Does everything in your home serve a specific purpose today? (Vague future purposes, like those recipes in a year-old magazine you swear to use someday, don't count.)

    e. Do you regret anything you've bought in the past year? (Think clothing, gadgets, household furniture and goods.)

    f. Does tax season give you headaches, indigestion, and maybe even the occasional panic attack?

    g. Do you own a shredder?

    h. Can you see yourself in five years? Ten years? And is that where you want to be?

Scoring:

1. a (2 points); b (1 point); c (0 points)
2. a (2 points); b (1 point); c (0 points)
3. a (2 points); b (1 point); c (0 points)
4. a (0 points); b (1 point); c (2 points)
5. a (0 points); b (1 point); c (2 points)
6. a (0 points); b (1 point); c (2 points)
7. a (2 points); b (1 point); c (0 points)
8. Give yourself 2 points each if you answered: (a) yes; (b) no; (c) no; (d) yes; (e) no; (f) no; (g) yes; and (h) yes.

The lower your score, the less control you have of your world. Conversely, the higher your score, the more control you have in your life.

If you scored below 10 points: you're barely holding on, and you probably worry so much about everything that you suffer health consequences, too. Nothing ever seems to go your way, and you're never on your own priority list. The thought of tackling your debt, financial paperwork, and clutter is downright terrifying. The word "money" makes you cringe. I'm guessing you hide the extent of the chaos pretty well from friends and family, but you know that if you don't get a handle on things soon, you're going to crack. "Happiness" is not a word you use very often. You can't remember the last time you felt young and energetic. You don't know what's good for you anymore because you've gotten so lost. And the dread of living like this for another day is practically unbearable. You have a lot of work to do, but the good news is that one little step can result in a giant leap forward. It may take time to get used to living by a new set of rules and perspective, but the exercises in this book will help you shift how you view your life, and learn to never let money or things run your life again.

If you scored between 11 and 20 points: your life needs a makeover, too, but you've got a better grip on things. You know you need to take action today or risk falling much farther down the hole. You do try hard to keep all the balls in the air, but your efforts aren't always working. The debt still lingers, the stuff still collects, the mind still wanders down depressive paths. More than likely money remains a big issue in your household. Despite what you know is good for you deep down, you still have problems with gaining control over what's important in your life, and avoiding or cleaning out the unimportant so you can stay attuned to your own desires and dreams. Happiness? You can't say whether or not you're truly happy because you've forgotten what that really means. You can be easily derailed, and when it comes to your kids, they rule. But you're aware of this, which is why a little bit more effort and focus can propel you to where you really want to be.

If you scored above 20 points: you get the gold star. You're lucky to be part of a small but growing group of people who work hard at maintaining their lives free of clutter, serious debt, and chaos. You were smart enough to set yourself up for the future and have made regular choices (sometimes hard ones) to maintain balance in your financial and personal lives. But that work requires constant vigilance and attention. You know how easy it can be to slip up and then have to pay the consequences—literally and figuratively. Happiness is elusive to some degree, but you sense that your priorities are in some semblance of order because you're feeling pretty good about yourself and your life. Money doesn't scare you, but you are very aware that can change on a dime. For you, this book will be a welcome reminder, and its fresh tips can help you to further fine-tune the good habits that keep you balanced and clutter free on all levels.

Dear Peter:
Going from two incomes to one was and still is quite a transition. However, we've been able to handle that transition quite well. We have gotten rid of many extra expenses, I buy used baby gear and clothes when I can, I cut coupons, use cloth diapers, and we're always looking for what else we can cut out. I have discovered that there is something very freeing in my spirit when I live a simpler life. I am finding that with less stuff, only the essentials and stuff that is truly important to me, it's a lot easier to clean my house and I actually am less stressed and able to spend more quality time with my family. It has made me reflect on times when life was simpler, too. We don't need extra storage garages or more stuff piled in the garage: we just need to honor and support our life with what matters most, and what matters most is not the stuff clogging up my closet!

IT STARTS WITH A VISION

If I had to give you one word that lies at the root of most people's emotional pain and anguish today, you'd probably be surprised it's not "money" (or the lack thereof). It's "stuff." Stuff keeps us from having the rich, full life we deserve. More stuff doesn't equate to a better life. Stuff has a way of creeping into and overtaking our homes. It also has a way of defining us, when we should be defining ourselves from a much deeper, intangible perspective. And when our stuff begins to define who we are, we become incapable of defining ourselves outside of what we own and what we can buy. This, as many of you may know by now, is a setup for utter unhappiness. One of my favorite quotes comes from the movie *Fight Club*: "The things you own end up owning you." It's a great quote, one that I use often and one that's really worth pondering. I can also extend that quote: "The things you own end up owning your *identity*."

It's time to seriously examine ourselves and our relationships with the money, people, and things in our lives—and the lack thereof. No one should feel stressed out when she opens the door to her own home or buys staples for living. No one has to. No one should feel like he has "nothing" when he can count on his loved ones, even when there's a *lack of* material possessions and money. Your home and your financial stability are within your control. Consider this: if your home is not providing you with a place of peace and calm, of focus and motivation; if your home is instead a major source of stress and anxiety in your life, then isn't it obvious that things are seriously out of balance? If your own home does not offer you some measure of nourishment and calm, where are you finding that peace? Chances are, nowhere! Your home should be the place where you escape all negative forces in the world. How you live in that home—eat, breathe, sleep, play, and connect with loved ones— should be the antidote to stress, not the cause.

To get to the heart of our financial problems, we have to reframe how we view what we own, what we buy, how we pay, what we can afford, and what will help us create the life we want for ourselves. This is about living mindfully within our means and it begins with a new perspective and a new mind-set about consuming less, living with less, and being happy with less—a mind-set that embraces the idea that happiness doesn't automatically come with more. This process must start with a clear vision of the life you want—not a debt number or credit score. Just a vision—your vision—and a big one at that.

LESS IS MORE

Let's be honest, the concept of less is far less attractive than the concept of more. Just that word "less" carries a boatload of negative connotations. Less drums up thoughts of not having enough, being a few dollars short, getting the short end of the stick, not functioning at 100 percent, missing something, lacking something, and so on. It implies hardship, deprivation, destitution, and poverty. But does it have to be a negative term? What does less mean to you?

Complete the following statements:

With less, I am afraid that: _____

_____

With less, I won't be able to: _____

_____

With less, my happiness is: _____

_____

Think for a moment about what automatically comes to mind when you think of you with less. Are you afraid that life won't be as pleasurable or rewarding? Does less mean you can't be happy? Does the very idea of less threaten your happiness? Will having less and living on less income mean you won't be living the life of your dreams? Why do you think this way? How is this so? What preconceived notions about "more" are clouding your definition of "less"?

Now let's turn this table around. Our cynical relationship with this word "less" is completely arbitrary. What if we chose to look at it from a different perspective? What if, for example, we couch "less" in terms that relate to abundance? Having less doesn't have to equate with being less, or missing anything. It can, in fact, result in the opposite effect of being more and having more—less of the things that cripple us or trip us up and more happiness, more simplicity, more relaxation, more satisfaction, more energy, more time, more joy, more order, more freedom, more flexibility, more opportunities, more of the things we truly value and need to live the life we want. This concept of "less" that will change our lives is less stress, less worry, less anxiety, less debt, less dissatisfaction, less frustration, less failure, less chaos, less dependence, less dysfunction in our relationships, and less feeling trapped in our financial instability and clutter-filled homes. When you look at it this way, less really can be more.

The shift from seeing less as a negative to less as a positive happens when we embrace the concept of less as an opportunity to be responsible and to be mindful consumers. It's about filling our souls rather than our physical space. It's about peace of mind rather than just more, more, more.

Dear Peter:
Every day I see what is happening to people all over the world. It is heartbreaking. We suffered a really tough time, but with a bit of downsizing and adjusting to a new way of life, our

new way of living is wonderful. We no longer go shopping without purpose. We wait to do supermarket shopping until it is absolutely necessary. The pantry is neat and tidy, and I have a menu planned with the ingredients I have available. Home cooking is in and the kids love the snacks and treats we home bake. It is great for our health also. When we want to go and "do" something, we often pack a picnic and go for a bike ride to a park or similar. We search out free activities and have discovered some real treasures.

We lost possessions but gained a stronger family unit. I wouldn't swap our life for anything.

Maybe the old adage is true. Perhaps less can lead to more. More happiness. Take a look at your home and picture having half the amount of stuff in it right now. What does that look like? How would that make you feel? If you're having trouble envisioning this, then close your eyes and picture your kitchen so tidy it could be featured in a magazine, your closets only halfway filled, your tabletops free of clutter and mail, your bedroom a spa-like sanctuary, and your home office worthy of a photograph for Pottery Barn just like that kitchen. Stay with this imagery. How far off is that picture from your current home? Then consider having fewer credit card statements and bills coming at you in the mail with late-payment fines and fees. Imagine never getting another credit card statement or bill that you couldn't fully pay off right then and there. You love getting your mail, in fact, because you get so much personal satisfaction from paying your bills in full and on time every month.

Now consider for a moment that you can step off the stress and financial treadmill that you're on by embracing the less rather than chasing the more. Just allow yourself that thought and consider what your life would be like if you weren't burdened with so much stuff. Answer the following quick questions:

With more stuff I have to: _____

_____

_____

With more stuff I am unable to: _____

_____

_____

With less stuff I am able to: _____

_____

_____

With less stuff I feel I can: _____

_____

_____

Let's think more about larger goals and dreams. If you could envision the perfect life you want for yourself, what would that entail? An oceanfront house? A small vacation cabin in the mountains of Montana? A studio in your garage so you could paint for hours every day? Enough money for yourself and to be generous and philanthropic to others? Frequently dining in fine restaurants? Driving a new car every few years? Paying off your mortgage and credit cards? Hosting an annual family reunion? Downsizing to a smaller home or an apartment? Spending three months of the year traveling the world? Retiring at age sixty? Starting a business? Putting your kids through college and graduate school without loans and acquiring debt? Just some peace of mind so you can stop worrying all the time?

A lot of people ask me about the difference between a goal and a dream. They are not the same. A dream is a fantasy that doesn't have a real basis in your reality. A goal, on the other hand, is a concrete destination—the result of a plan and specific objective. It's fine to dream, as some dreams can and do become realities with the right goals in place beforehand, but in order to make your dreams real, you have to set and meet clear goals. Dreams are the fantasy long shots—like winning the lottery. Goals are the short-term milestones that you can achieve—like paying off your credit card bills—that can bring you closer to your ultimate dream.

Large or small, you have to know what you want in order to achieve it. You've probably been told this all your life, but you have to set goals and decide what you want before going after them. Without a roadmap, how can you ever know that you've reached your destination? Let's try another exercise that I use with my clients. You're going to ask yourself some questions about the life you want. Feel free to ask other people their opinions also if you like, for what you hear from others can help inform your own vision. The only requirement here is that you aim to be as specific as possible, and within reason. Let your imagination run loose, but be sure these goals are achievable. For example, rather than say you want to "be skinny and have millions of dollars to spend on designer clothes," shift that statement to "reach my ideal weight where I'm healthy and have enough money to meet my shopping interests without going into debt or compromising my family."

Take your time here. Don't be hesitant or afraid. Go for it. Describe for me your best, reasonable lifestyle (and don't factor in winning the lottery!). You can use full sentences or just words, terms, descriptors, and lists. Think about your life in all its dimensions:

financial goals, career/business goals, free time/family time, health/ appearance goals, relationship goals, personal growth, and making a difference. I recommend writing down at least three goals in each of these categories. If you're in a relationship, it helps to do this exercise with your partner.

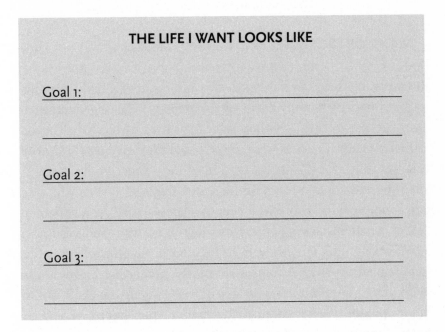

THE LIFE I WANT LOOKS LIKE

Goal 1: _____

_____

Goal 2: _____

_____

Goal 3: _____

_____

Was this exercise easy or hard for you? I'll bet your mind was racing with all kinds of thoughts, hopes, and wants. It's difficult when you have to focus on what matters and what you want from your life. When you think about it, maybe you realize that the dream house on the hill isn't really what you see for yourself. Or perhaps that's exactly what you do want (with the passport to Europe once a year). Writing down and clarifying your desires and setting goals are the first step toward achieving them. Then committing to the life you want by starting today to make conscious, mindful decisions that move you closer to that goal.

You'll frequently return to this section to measure how close you are to reaching your goals. Your vision may change as you go through the process and you may after all decide, "Nah, that's not really want I want. What on earth was I thinking?" or "Wow, I really believe I can do this!" As I take you through all the steps in this book, you'll find yourself modifying, developing, expanding, and shaping your vision into its final form.

FOR LIFE OR FROM LIFE?

It's amazing the difference one little word can make. Early on in my career I noticed that my clients were constantly talking about what they needed to make their homes or their lives perfect. The conversation was always about what they needed *for* their homes. "I need a larger couch for this room" or "I need more room for my clothes" or "We need another room for my craft supplies." It seems that we are conditioned to think in terms of what we need *for* a situation. We're constantly asking ourselves what do we want and need *for* a comfortable life? The answers usually have something to do with acquiring more stuff. A comfortable life might mean a bigger house with more room for the family and all the goodies you get to buy to fill it up. More money means better hotels when you travel, fancier restaurants and costlier wines when you dine out, or better seats at concerts and sporting events.

But try a different exercise. Before asking the "what do I need for" question, ask what do you want *from* a situation? What do you want *from* your master bedroom? What do you want *from* your family room? What do you want *from* your relationship? What do you want *from* your home and your life? Changing that one small word—*for* to *from*—helps you gain a whole new perspective on what you own, what you buy and what you think is important in your life.

In the previous exercise, I gave you some big categories under which to think about the vision you have for yourself. With those in mind, ask yourself what you want from each of those critical areas in your life:

- What do I want FROM my financial life? _____

_____

- What do I want FROM my career? _____

_____

- What do I want FROM my free (*me*) time? _____

_____

- What do I want FROM my family time? _____

_____

- What do I want FROM a healthy life? _____

_____

- What do I want FROM my relationships? _____

_____

- What do I want FROM my personal growth? _____

_____

Do any of your responses above match your answers in 'The Life I Want Looks Like' exercise on page 31? How are they different? And how do your responses here help you to modify that vision?

Another question you may want to ask yourself is, What will people say about me when I am gone? How will they describe me? What kind of legacy will I leave?

Remember that you are beginning a process that will help you change the way you see your life, the things you own, and what brings you happiness. I'm here to help you figure out what's truly important and what holds meaning for your life—the foundation for your happiness. You've already taken a huge step in outlining a rough vision for yourself. So let's get going with making that vision a reality.

Dear Peter:

In learning to stem the flow of input, the result has been time and energy to deal with a lot of things that have accumulated. I remind myself that every item has come into my house with my permission. Stopping it before it crosses the threshold by not buying it in the first place is beginning to be internalized by me.

Slowing down the speed of life gives you time to discern what is of value to you. It gives opportunity to reflect on where you are, where you are going, and maybe adjust the direction you journey is taking.

This gets down to past, present, and future. What area of my life is this item for/from? A recession is the best thing that could happen to the war on clutter.

When most people think of clutter they think of the stuff that fills their garage or closets, of all those things strewn across kitchen countertops, and the flood of paperwork that seems insurmountable. If that's your concept of clutter I need you to think much more broadly. In the work that I do clutter means *anything* that stands between you and the vision you have for your best life—it's so much more than just the stuff. Those repeated bad decisions you make in your relationship? Clutter. Your anger and anxiety at work? Clutter. That voice in your head that tells you you're not worthy of happiness? Clutter. The thoughts and feelings that constantly say you don't deserve to be happy? Clutter. The fear and self-loathing that consume your days now that life ain't what it used to be when money was abundant? Clutter. The decisions that have landed you in financial hell? Clutter. This is the definition of clutter that I embrace in my work and in this book. It could be a pile of inherited furniture or a jumble of kids' toys all over the living room. But it could also be the constant self-doubt that creeps into your decision making; anger about how you're not able to pay every bill each month; frustration about how you're treated at work; shame about not being confident about the future; or a tendency to respond defensively and critically when your spouse challenges you.

And so to deal with any clutter—in your home, your head, or your heart—you have to start not with the clutter itself but with this perennial question: What is the vision you have for the life (or home, or relationship, or body, or family, or financial health) you want? Once you start pondering this question your whole perspective begins to shift and a level of mindfulness is introduced into every aspect of your life.

Another way to find the answer to this question is to ask yourself: Where do I derive happiness? Let's find out in the next chapter.

2

What Makes You Happy?

Everyone values, saves, and understands the role of money in life a bit differently, just as everyone responds differently to money, or the lack of it. No two money personalities are exactly the same. By the time we're adults, most of us have established a unique set of ingrained money habits as well as a certain tolerance for taking on debt. We've developed our own "money personality." Some of us mature into savers and err on the side of caution, while others grow into spenders and seize every single day by opening their wallet. Some of us feel intimidated and scared to death by money while others are able to remove all emotion from the matter. And some of us live in denial by avoiding basic money management skills as others wise up and learn how to create a budget, invest, and avoid impulsive spending sprees.

None of us is born with an innate sense of how to handle money successfully, but we learn through our parents, peers, culture, teachers, and good old trial and error. When times are good and the economy is flush, we fail to consider the repercussions of buying on credit and letting debt build up. When times are not so good and money gets tight, though, the reverse happens. Suddenly, we are acutely aware of debt's downsides. We begin to regret our spending sprees and fear the mailman because all he brings is bad news in the form of bills and late notices. Our access lines to more borrowed money get cut, and it feels like we're being strangled. The longer we lived high on the hog, the harder it became to shift gears and learn to live on less.

Prior to the recent financial fallout, all of us were on a wild ride in a booming economy. People of all income levels joined the party and most of us were happily living beyond our means loading up on things and debt we didn't need. There was little thought about the hangover the next day. There was little talk about the what-ifs that tomorrow would bring. In looking back, most of us realize that we should have been more cautious. Regretting the past, however, is a waste of time. Now's the time to shift course and make the proper adjustments so you can move forward with a much more promising, secure future that won't look anything like what you're currently experiencing. That movement forward, though, starts with a lesson you learned long ago, but have forgotten. It's the one about needs versus wants. Our spending orgy evicted the definitions of these words from our vocabulary, and we must bring them back into full focus. And full acceptance.

Dear Peter:
About a year ago the bank cut my house-flipping business off completely. I am sixty years young and had been doing this most of my adult life. Credit card limits kept shrinking, and the interest rate went up as high as 33 percent on some cards. Using your principles has been a godsend. Favorite one . . . Is this a WANT or a NEED? It has been a struggle but I have learned to live on only what I have in the bank. No more credit cards, no more buying new . . . I use Goodwill for my career

wardrobe . . . garage sales for any kitchen gadgets, etc. I may need. Our Christmas this year is going GREEN, which is giving recycled items that are brand new just never used.

This morning I finished the job of clean sweeping my walk-in closet. I feel so much lighter and in control of my life in general. I really cannot describe the feeling but I want to thank you from the bottom of my heart for all of your practical ideas and approaches to ridding our lives of clutter.

NEEDS VERSUS WANTS VERSUS ENTITLEMENTS

This chapter is going to ask you to differentiate your wants from your needs and really clarify how they enforce or hurt that vision you have for yourself. This will entail taking an honest look at what you think makes you happy and how the items you've amassed over the years have affected your financial and emotional well-being. Let's start by making some important distinctions. Needs are what you require to survive. Wants are everything else, including the things you *think* you require to survive or make yourself feel good. And entitlements are often misguided beliefs we carry about what we think we have a *right* to have or own. There's definitely something to be said for needs that enhance our quality of life. But all too often we let a sense of entitlement vandalize a decent amount of reasonable wants. For example, food is a necessity. But a monthly food bill in the thousands of dollars for shopping at the priciest markets and dining at the finest restaurants is not. Likewise, shelter and clothing are necessities. But having the biggest house on the block and a walk-in closet filled with designer fashions are not.

That said, I won't ask you to eject every single want. I'm just asking you to rein in and adjust your wants to make sure that each one is contributing toward the life you imagine for yourself and your family. I'm also asking that you redefine what you feel you're entitled to, and how you go about getting that.

But before we even get to your life specifically, I want to address the white elephant that sits in a lot of people's homes and continues to drive us down dangerous paths that end in financial hardship, anguish, and, of course, unhappiness. That big hairy elephant is called consumption: the purchasing of goods and services, or, more specifically, the *over*purchasing of goods and services. I find it ironic how centuries ago, when people died of tuberculosis, they were said to have "died of consumption," referring to the way the disease wasted away one's energy from within. That perspective couldn't be closer to the truth when it comes to the consumption of too many goods and services. Consumption doesn't just consume our energy and bank account, it consumes our happiness and our chances of achieving peace and calm in our lives.

WHY CONSUMPTION DEVOURS CONTENTMENT

If you were to calculate how many times during the day you are exposed to persuasive ads about consuming, you would be astounded. The number would likely be in the thousands, including those microseconds that your eyes spend scanning website pages filled with ads or unconsciously consuming the message on the billboards that clutter most roadways in America. Just taking the number of ads that motivate you to seek food alone is incredibly revealing. The average American is exposed to about 3,900 calories a day through TV, radio, and print ads. Studies have proven that the more we see food, the more we want to eat it. The ability of advertisers to convince you of the need to buy their products is no less seductive. Companies are now resorting to very sophisticated "neuromarketing" to analyze brain wave patterns and the body's chemical responses to various stimuli to help them accurately predict which products will succeed and fail with consumers. Increasingly, our decision to buy is finessed, manipulated, and controlled by forces we are only dimly aware of.

The job of marketers is to sell you on the idea that if you buy their product you will be *happier* and somehow better than you are. Ad slogans across the board exploit our desire to be happier, healthier, and safer. They also cater to our aspirations. Take a look at some of the more popular brands' slogans:

- Visa: It's everywhere you want to be.
- Nokia: Connecting people.
- Burger King: Have it your way.
- Kohl's: Expect great things.
- L'Oréal: Because I'm worth it.
- Time Warner Cable: The power of you.

Who doesn't want to be connected with people, have it their way, expect great things, be worth it, and be more powerful? Of course achieving all of this would make us happier, bigger, brighter, smarter, better looking and generally more fabulous than we are now! No wonder we congregate in malls. That's where I'll find the better version of me I've been searching for! But when we buy into these powerful messages and promises, we aren't guaranteed the implied result. We can easily end up throwing money at promises that don't deliver, and in doing so distance ourselves farther from the promises we've made to ourselves, such as the promise to be more fiscally responsible. In any year, more than two-thirds of the households in this country spend a sizeable portion of their disposable income on goods and services that tend to be disposable themselves—in other words, they gobble up our money quickly but don't retain our interest for long. These include things like videos, CDs, DVDs, magazines, personal care products, crafting supplies, and candles. Other items—like cars or electronics—lose a huge portion of their purchase price the moment we pay for them.

It doesn't help that our government adds its own stamp of approval on consumption when it uses consumer spending as a vital sign of our nation's well-being. Consumerism is seen as the benchmark of our nation's economic health. We constantly hear about the state of our economy based on consumer figures—how much people are spending, how the retailers are faring, and what those future projections are. This is not health but the chasing of a promise that has somehow been tied to the concept of national happiness. The implication is that if we're not spending, not consuming, then we're just not healthy. It's even been suggested that if we're not spending, we're not good citizens. After the terrorist attacks of 9/11, politicians repeatedly told us that one of the best things we could do to help ourselves recover was to go out and spend money. Our nation depended on it! So when our leaders and the people we look up to for advice and guidance are telling us that spending money is a good thing for our country—a defining thing for our country—and that our lives and livelihoods depend on it, is there any wonder why we don't stop to question that strategy? How can we say no when the powers that be cry out "yes, yes, yes, spend, spend, spend"?

I know, it's very hard to say no when the world in which we live seems to tell us to literally (to use yet another popular slogan) *just do it*. In the heat of thinking about, anticipating, and planning our purchases we actually do feel empowered, but how long does that really last? How many times have you spent money you didn't have on an outfit, a gadget, or a home improvement product that was going to change your life only to have it lose its appeal within days of bringing it home?

I will say that a lot of this behavior is part of our DNA, and not just a recent phenomenon. Back when we were hunters and gatherers, the rewards that came with finding food for survival did, in fact, assure our survival. It feels good to buy something—to acquire something we think we need to stay alive. We get a psychological lift that's rooted in a physical reaction in the body as the feel-good endorphins bathe our brain and satisfy its pleasure center. Shopping also

41

satisfies another need that dates back to our caveman days—that of socializing with others. We are social beings, and the act of going to the marketplace even just to look and be around other people is a very human experience grounded in our evolutionary history. But the problem we seem to have with "retail therapy" lately is that it's far too easy to engage in shopping and abuse our innate wiring for "gathering." Opportunities to shop abound today like never before. You would be hard-pressed to travel five miles without coming across someplace to shop and buy something, even if it's just at a gas station or roadside store. Closer still is online shopping, with links to retailers around the globe who'll deliver to our homes, 24/7. The same can be said for the food industry. Our bodies have fundamentally remained unchanged for millennia, but not our access to food. We used to have to work hard to acquire food to eat, and now it's at our fingertips whenever we desire it.

Which is what makes taking control of shopping, or eating for that matter, so hard. It seems to go against our inherent needs and wants. When we force ourselves to avoid the mall or put down that delicious doughnut, our bodies cry out because we haven't evolved yet to deal with our modern world of unlimited shops and food. If you've ever noticed that you shop or eat when you're bored or looking for a pick-me-up, you can thank our ancient DNA. The body knows it can get a boost from a trip to the mall and a leisurely half hour at the food court.

So is there a way to combat this force of nature? Of course, because the brain is a powerful organ and you can retrain it to think and to respond in a different way. Change is difficult, even when it's essential to our survival. But understanding the need for this change can help us make the sacrifices necessary and enable us to find motivation.

Remember, the more you have the more you have to maintain, watch out for, order, clean, service, take care of, worry about, spend time on, throw money at, and so on and so forth. This all amounts to less time spent on the truly important things in your life, like family, relationships, and yourself—the very things that contribute to your sense of well-being and happiness. Here's another way to look at it: Visa likes to say that it's everywhere you want to be, but if you've maxed out your Visa privileges (because you do take it everywhere you want to be and use it everywhere you are), then consider for a moment what you're left with—the heartache of constantly facing those bills, the anguish and self-hatred for letting the card facilitate too many mindless purchases, and the time and energy you will "spend" dealing with the debt, the creditors, the family members affected by your habit, and the future of your and your family's financial life. Credit cards easily give you the false impression that there are no limits, but I'm sure you know by now that limits do exist. They always have. They always will. The better you can honor and respect those limits in the context of your own life, the better off you will be. And trust me, the happier you will be.

Speaking of time and energy, it's worth noting that one of the top five complaints doctors get these days is lack of energy. When I poll people about their dreams—what they want most—more time and more energy are frequently at the top of that list. Time and energy are not things we can easily quantify like we can debt or possessions, but they carry enormous weight in our clutter equation. Like our relationships, our spirituality, and the love we share with others, time and energy are intangible. We cannot touch, see, or feel time or energy, but we definitely see and feel the effects when we don't have enough of them.

EXPLORING YOUR LIMITS

In life, there are limits. We can't all climb Mt. Everest. We can't all live in mansions with butlers and drive Rolls-Royces. We can't all have an unlimited source of funds just as we can't have unlimited natural resources. On planet Earth there are limitations to be had despite desires, wants, entitlements, and wishes. And despite your best efforts.

Limits are all around us. We have a limited number of hours in the day. We only have so many days in a year, and so many years in a life. Limits exist in other, less numerical, areas of life as well, such as a limited amount of strength, limited tolerance for physical pain, ability to only run so fast, and even a limit to patience before we lose our cool. Although many of our limits are elastic, meaning they tend to be flexible and can be stretched with our conscious efforts, there are absolute limits beyond which we cannot go. In fact challenging our limits often helps us grow and become more evolved human beings. But we still have to acknowledge our limits for our own safety and well-being. It does us no good to blindly force our limits without if we don't understand and appreciate the potential consequences. And this is especially true with regard to the limits of space, money, time, and energy.

Resisting or pushing limits is not necessarily a bad thing but pretending they don't exist is a serious mistake. Acknowledging and embracing your limits—financial or otherwise—can provide a clarity and focus that will keep you firmly rooted in reality. My guess is that right now the life you have been living cannot be supported by your financial reality; otherwise, it's unlikely you'd be reading this book. But that's okay. I want to help you look at how you have been living, examine it carefully, and readjust or recalibrate where necessary. The exercises that follow will also help you look at the time, effort, and resources you're dedicating to maintain what could be a flawed or unrealistic vision for the life you're pursuing. Because, despite all the sexy and alluring ads and slogans, which lured you on the ill-fated voyage to where you are today, you're not happier. You're not where you want to be. Let's begin to change that.

WHERE DO YOU DERIVE HAPPINESS?

A solid starting point is to assess what it means for you to be happy. To do this section, you need to find your favorite place to sit and think, away from distractions, and really wrap your brain around the following exercise. Be honest when you write down your answers. It won't work if you're not 100 percent honest!

THE HAPPINESS FACTOR

- What do I value the most? _____

_____

_____

- What is my greatest treasure? _____

_____

_____

- What can't be replaced? _____

_____

_____

- What makes me happy? _____

_____

_____

- When am I happiest? _____

_____

_____

- When am I unhappiest? _____

_____

_____

- If I had to list one or two things that would make me
  happier today, they would be: _____

_____

_____

My guess is that words and ideas popped into your head that had nothing to do with tangible things or money. Did the health of your family trump your big-screen TV? Did your love for your kids beat out your love for clothes and jewelry? Did spending time with a loved one on the couch win over a trip to the mall alone? We usually think of possessions and money creating happiness but it's actually the intangibles that we value more when it comes down to it. I remember reading after the devastating wildfires in California a couple of years ago that some people spoke of their renewed perspective. Even though they'd lost everything, they had managed to save themselves, their families, and their pets. They were most grateful that those they loved were safe, even in the face of devastating material loss. I'm not suggesting that anyone should ever go through such a trauma to gain a new perspective, but there is a lesson in this for us all.

What's also remarkable is that people who endure such losses often speak of wealth and riches in totally new terms afterward. In other words, if you were to ask victims of a tremendous tragedy if they feel rich or wealthy following the incident, they would say yes. They are rich in spirit and they are wealthy in reality. Why? Because in their new reality, they have everything they need to feel alive and well. They derive wealth not from their possessions or big houses, but from the people they love, who bring them joy, and who are still with them.

Dear Peter:
Almost a year ago my husband was laid off. It was frustrating and scary. We weren't sure what to do about work, and it was clear no one was hiring. We eat at home more often now, which has had the benefit of us getting creative, making menus and eating healthier for less money. We look back at this past year, and see how with our children aged twelve and fourteen we've spent so much more time as a family.

With less money, but more time, we are more organized and have time for conversations and hiking. We eat healthier and then exercise more with the hikes. We are helping charity organizations more than ever. While our donations are not monetary, they are useful items or our time. This time spent volunteering also bonds us as a family since we do it together. It feels much better than going to the mall ever did! We not only have a great time, but we make our community better at the same time.

Now we know where everything is that we need/want. We feel good knowing others are enjoying the items we do not want/need. We have space and time, which is so much better than before. While we are a bit stressed about money since it is in short supply, we are actually enjoying life more regardless of that added stress. The extra time we have and the things we've chosen to do with that time now mean so much more! We are less tired as we are getting more sleep, too!

We hope for more stable employment and full-time employment sooner than later. However, we're taking advantage of the gift of time as a family and taking time to have a life together.

Just as we need to get clear on what makes us happy, we also need to be honest about what it means to be wealthy. Far too often the word "wealth" relates to money, social status, and possessions—perpetuated by the media and amplified by celebrity gossip. I want you to try and see wealth not as a tally of valuables or a stock portfolio, but rather a barometer of inner peace and contentment. Given this definition, "wealthy" means you are healthy, happy, and safe.

As you read through the rest of this book, keep this definition of wealth in mind. Wherever you derive your happiness from—and for most of us it's a combination of family, intimate relationships, friendships, career pursuits, and passions—make it a goal to focus on those sources. See if you can move away from focusing on the things you *think* you need to be happy, and instead concentrate on the people, passions, and pursuits that you know bring you joy. If it helps, keep the list you wrote out of what makes you truly happy posted nearby as you complete the exercises in this book. Your sources of happiness are what ultimately drive your vision forward. They are what inspire you to change. They are what will allow you to take a good hard look at your possessions and identify and move past the false sense of security and happiness they seem to provide.

PLANNING, NOT ORGANIZING

Before we actually begin to attack all of your metaphorical piles of clutter and deepest emotional hang-ups, I want to make one thing very clear: this is not about "getting organized" in the traditional sense—mentally or physically. Whether you have real piles of clutter to deal with or just imagined ones in your head that revolve around your emotional compass, I want you to move way beyond the "getting organized." Remember, this book is totally different from any other you've read before, including my own. The work we're doing here is not about how best to label file folders or how long to keep paperwork. It's not even about tracking down the best interest rates or what financial institution has the most attractive investment portfolios. No—we're starting with something far more fundamental. I want you to step back from the "getting organized" idea and replace it with something exceedingly more basic to your financial health: *planning for the full, happy life you want to live.* This is about making room for the vision you have for yourself. This is about going far beyond the physical and material possessions and addressing those underlying assumptions and mind-sets that infiltrate not just your house but also your psyche. We're about to take a serious inventory of you and where you're at now, and begin to map that reality against your vision so you develop a real, practical plan.

I SEE, I WANT, I BUY

We've all done it. We see something we like, we feel a gotta-have-it rush, and we buy it. No questions asked. Until *now.*

Once you are aware of the vision you have for the life you want, the see-want-buy process is going to stop. You will no longer (and I mean it: you really will no longer) go from see to want to buy in an instant. You will see something, want it, but then pause to ask yourself: Will this thing (or action or word or decision) move me closer to the vision I have for the life I want? If the answer is yes, then if you can afford it you may give yourself permission to go ahead and buy that particular thing. If the answer is no, then you will ask yourself why you thought you wanted to buy it in the first place. The process makes buying take on a whole new meaning. What you choose to purchase no longer is based on price, or impulse, or that caveman mentality; it becomes an action taken on a much deeper level of mindfulness and awareness. You will even come to see the things you already own in a whole new light, and may even find that some of your existing possessions can be a source of happiness that a newly purchased item cannot match.

"Does this item or thought or response move me closer to my vision for my best life?" This is a simple question but one with a profound impact on your habits and your life, and only you can answer it honestly. If your answer is no, why would you want to own something that prevents you from realizing your best life? I guarantee that if you introduce this level of mindfulness into your decisions it will transform the way you live. It will introduce a level of consideration and mindfulness into your purchases that did not exist before. It will also allow you to say no and then walk away feeling a tremendous amount of power, control, and yes, happiness.

The caveat, though, is that this new process only works with a very clear vision that you wholeheartedly believe in. Your vision needs to be bigger than any single item you want to buy or action, word, or decision you want to make. If you still don't have that vision ringing loud and clear for you, then I encourage you to go back to Chapter 1 and take your time to map that vision out. Don't fool yourself into thinking a half-baked vision will help you complete the upcoming exercises truthfully. You cannot cheat your way through this with a semi, maybe, almost, not-really-sure kind of vision.

THE AUDITS: WHERE YOU CURRENTLY STAND

When I work with people who either have their own small business or work for a retail company, I ask them about the annual event
when their stores close down to take inventory. Why do they do this?
What's the point of losing business for a day or so to take the pulse
of the company's supplies and bookkeeping? Virtually all shops and
businesses take a time-out on at least an annual basis to pay attention to themselves rather than focusing on customers and orders.
This allows them to see what state their business is in, catalog their
inventory, analyze whether or not past strategies have helped or hurt
their bottom line, and what actions they should now take to ensure
the future health of the business.

Company inventories and audits give the people who run those
companies the knowledge they need to instigate necessary change,
to plan new strategies, and to discern what has worked and what
hasn't. Why, though, do we participate in these highly revealing and
helpful inventories and audits in our working lives but don't think
about doing the same for our personal lives? If they are essential to
the health and success of companies, then why can't we do the same
for ourselves?

Taking a personal inventory is much more difficult because
we're not objectively counting somebody else's goods; we're counting our own private possessions, dollars, and "sense." We're con-
fronting our own past mistakes, poor decisions, and misguided
strategies. It's almost impossible to conduct a personal audit without
being overwhelmed by the emotions that are tied up in our findings.
So as we audit our lives, we simultaneously find ourselves auditing
our memories, feelings (some of which can be unexpected), aspirations, and disappointments.

And that's okay. In fact, it's more than okay. Dealing with these
feelings and fears is a necessary rite of passage to reaching your vision. The upcoming audits are going to be tough for some of you, but
I promise that they will do more for you and your future than you

ever imagined. They will help you to see exactly where you are and give you a chance to take stock of your life, as well as where you're going.

The Big Three: Emotions, Money, and the Stuff

I have three audits for you to do, and what I love about these audits is that they will really audit everything about you. Not just your financial life and possessions, but also your emotional junk, your time, your energy, your tolerance, your risk taking, your priorities, your *sanity*. Far too often I watch people go through financial checkups—they haul out their bills and bank statements, begin to prioritize debt according to a financial expert's rules, attempt to battle the credit card companies over interest rates, and then white-knuckle their way through creating another new budget and another new savings plan they then try to stick to. These efforts are valiant but usually fail because in the background all that other stuff—the self-doubt, the anxiety, the shame, the guilt, the lack of time, the "whatever emotional hang-up" they harbor—continues to pile up and erode their well-being. And it always seems to bring them right back to where they started from.

The following three audits should give you a complete 360-degree picture of your life:

1. Personal audit: What emotional stuff have you assumed that's affecting your life?
2. Financial audit: What financial stuff have you taken on that's affecting your life?
3. Home audit: What physical stuff have you filled your home with that's affecting your life?

By assessing each of these three areas of your life you'll be in a better position to see where you are and to gauge how far you are from where you want to be. You'll also be able to see what's standing between you and where you want to be. Your clutter may not be the same as your friend's or neighbor's, but it's clutter nonetheless. Once you have identified which "clutter" is littering your life, you'll be poised to deal with it once and for all.

Each audit has two parts: First you'll get a chance to audit a certain area of your life and consider the exact vision you have for that area. And, in fact, we'll be working on those visions first because how you see your life and the spaces you occupy will dictate how you proceed to clean up that life and those spaces. Put simply, how you envision your life must come before anything else, no matter how overwhelming or pressing that "everything else" seems to be. Then, once we have both the clear vision and a sense of today's reality, we'll be more able to see the gap between "the real and the ideal." Only then will you be in a position to make the necessary adjustments so you can move closer to achieving your ideal.

In the second part of each audit, we'll actually begin to tackle what you uncover in these audits little by little, space by space. But for now, keep an open mind and let your imagination kick into high gear. Try to put on a special pair of glasses that will allow you to really see what you find when I ask you to take a hard look at your surroundings, your feelings, and your vision. Surrender your fears and respond to these audits as honestly as possible. There are no right or wrong answers but honesty is key if you really want this to work. Again, for some of you, this may be a grueling experience. Emotions may surface that you never thought were there. That's okay. In fact, that's essential to this entire process. If your emotional response gets to be too overwhelming, and you just don't know how to handle it, stop and take a break. Talk with someone you trust or try writing in a journal about what you're feeling and remind yourself this process paves your way to a better, brighter future. You're human if you become bombarded by mixed emotions. In fact, I expect you to confront uncomfortable feelings, so do what you can to embrace them rather than push them away or avoid them. Troubling emotions can actually be a source of strength and motivation.

We'll start with the broadest audit of all by just considering *you*—your psychological underpinnings. What makes you tick. If you need to steal a slogan to cheer you on as you go forward and face the music, then I suggest you repeat the following when you find yourself asking Why am I doing this again? Answer: *because you're worth it*. You, your family, your future, and your dreams are all worth it!

part two

From Audit to Action

The Personal Audit: Your Life

FROM THE MOMENT WE ARE BORN, we start to acquire. In fact, this starts sooner than our original birthday—it starts in the womb. Early images of babies in utero can be seen sucking their thumbs and gripping their little hands. It's human instinct; from the beginning we want to draw things toward us and hold on to them. Think about it: it's much easier to clench or grip your hands than to keep your palms open wide. The most comfortable posture for the resting hand is to curl in on itself. To have and to hold has a positive ring to it; to relinquish, renounce, release, and give up all sound negative and unappealing.

I see this need to grasp things played out every day when I work with people trying to clear out their clutter—trying to let go so on another level they can welcome more into their life. Given the new reality that we've all encountered in the last couple of years, many of us have been forced to let go and give up things we've had (and perhaps cherished) in the past. The connection between things and money and us and our things has never been more pronounced than it is today. That connection defines who we are, and where we think we want to be. When I started working on this book, I asked people to share with me how they were dealing with the financially challenging times. Every response offered great ideas for cutting back (quit the gym and join a community recreation center, stop buying designer coffee and make it at home), spending less on entertainment (use the library for books and DVDs), thinking about money (saving money despite debt), and getting rid of unnecessary, unfulfilling stuff (selling semi-valuable possessions like electronics and high-end clothing and accessories online).

That's all well and good, but not one answer was about the emotional connection to money. So I sent out another email, this time asking people if they felt any differently about money. I asked, Do you feel deprived? Angry? Happier? Resentful? Stressed? Nothing? Everything?

Boy, did my email box fill up quickly! I think we all can relate to these responses:

Suspicious. "I don't trust money anymore. It seems to be a mirage— is it real? The good thing about the recession is that it has made me consider every purchase and whether it's really necessary. And that has forced me to save for rainy days."

Scared. "I felt downright scared, like ice was running through my veins, when the Dow kept hitting new lows and deal after deal (I'm a real estate agent) kept falling apart."

Resentful. "I don't resent having to make changes—change can be good. But it doesn't always turn out well. I'm resentful because of having worked so hard all my life and now it's rendered futile."

Worried. "I've cut back on everything—eating out, groceries, gifts, gas, shopping. But will I ever be able to retire? I don't see it happening—ever. I can't sleep at night and my health has taken a serious hit."

Grateful. "This period has been a good learning experience for me and I hope I don't go back to spending frivolously. Ever."

Frustrated. "It's frustrating to see some people and companies bailed out big time, but come April 15, I'm still going to owe Uncle Sam a big chunk of change."

How many of these statements sound like the voice inside your own head? Did any one of these really hit home for you? Which one?

You've got plenty of company. Even if you still have your job and it's secure, no doubt recent financial changes have compelled you to view money—and your financial situation—differently. It's all well and good to cut back, save, and spend less. But that doesn't necessarily mean you enjoy doing it. The needy infant in all of us is simply human nature.

That need for more is what compounds all those negative feelings you have about your lack of money. Not having the amount we really want—or *think* we want—to live the life we think we deserve is stressing us out and alienating us from our partners, our families, and our dreams. We have all bought too easily and too quickly into the Myth of More. We can only be happier if we have more than we possess and the more costly and special the item, the more important and special we are for owning it. Happiness has become an exercise in comparison with those around us. If they have more, then it stands to reason they must be happier. So, our logic goes, to be happier we have to have more. This circular argument, not based in reality, has been a huge contributor to our current situation. The irony is that if our happiness is based on comparing ourselves with the situation of others, we can never attain happiness. There will always be people who have more than we have. But remember, there will also always be people who have less, too.

We've been led to believe that if we can just acquire the right things then we can also acquire the life we want. We're caught up in the pursuit of the right house, the right car, the right furnishings, the right schools, the right restaurant reservations, the right vacation, the right labels, and on and on. Our energies become directed toward filling our homes with the "right" things so we can become the "right" kind of people. Once our focus shifts from the quality of our lives or relationships to the quantity of stuff we can acquire, we risk bringing into our lives not just an overwhelming quantity of material goods but also the worry and heartache that come with the costs involved in acquiring (and keeping) those goods. Instead of bringing you closer to the life you want to live, your worries and attitudes about the things you have (or need to have) and the money you must have in order to maintain and sustain the life you've created become a constant source of worry and stress in your daily life.

In the previous section, I asked you to think about the vision you have for yourself and your life. Now it's time to sync that vision with your personal circumstances, and begin to make sense of the disconnect between what you think you want, and, given your situation, what's possible.

PERSONAL AUDIT

Even though I haven't specifically asked you to take stock of your emotions up to this point of the book, I'm sure they've started to surface. The "Is This You?" quiz you took on pages 19–22 may have helped you identify the underlying emotional issues you have regarding your finances, your stuff, and your life. You may have released some deep-seated feelings you have about your life and your financial standing. Has anything I've covered thus far triggered a strong emotion like anger, regret, or bliss? Are you feeling mad, moody, or immobilized by what's going on in your mind?

Take a deep breath. If you weren't feeling a little bit of something at this point, you wouldn't be human. I work with people all the time who think they can take an objective look at themselves and their stuff but stay totally detached from their emotions. But it never happens. I also work with couples all the time who don't believe their relationship has a problem until we start to wade through the stuff and explore their assets and collective financial burdens among their bills. The stress of keeping up appearances—struggling to maintain a high standard of living on a less-than-high income—slowly leaks out. Indeed, it's stressful having to maintain all this stuff and pray you can pay all your bills next month. It's hard to be nice when you're constantly thinking about your troubled financial life and the fact that the future of your family could depend on your current habits.

Money may be the main reason people get divorced in this country. For couples trying to make ends meet, lack of money is an incredible source of tension. But tension over money is typically just a symptom of other pressures going on in the life of each individual. And the only way to move forward is to expose and examine those other pressures. So it is with this in mind that we now turn to the first official audit. Again, I'm not recommending this audit for purposes of making you feel like a bad person or to drag you through the mud. This three-phase audit is similar to a checkup of your health and has a very specific goal and a very effective outcome. It will help you identify the subconscious attitudes and beliefs behind your habits and behaviors, and understand which ones are either moving you closer to or farther away from your vision. Ready?

Personal Audit Phase I: Ask the Question

Remove dollar signs, objects, and household things from your mind. If you're sitting in your home right now and ruminating over the rooms and their contents, or your bills and those late notices, get out of your house and find a neutral place where you can focus solely on this audit. Maybe it's a seat in your backyard or a local coffee shop for half an hour. Bring a piece of paper and pen.

Wherever you choose to take this audit, make sure you are comfortable, free to think and write down whatever comes to mind, and won't be distracted or interrupted. Once you're in your special spot, get out that piece of paper and pen and answer the following question: **What is the source of the tension in your life?**

The answer can be any number of things. It could be the strained relationship you have with your spouse, your boss, your teenage son, or a friend. It could be the pain you suffer from negotiating with creditors every day as you attempt to save your small business. It could be the struggle you've gone through to lose weight and gain better health and energy. It could be the dissatisfaction you have at work and the path your career has taken. And it could be any combination of these things and more. In fact, our relationships with others and with ourselves play such a large role in our overall happiness quotient that it helps to stop and consider the following:

You and
. . . your partner.
. . . your kids.
. . . your parents.
. . . your family.
. . . your best friend.
. . . your boss.
. . . your co-workers.
. . . yourself.

Below is a chart to help you take a detailed inventory of the tensions. Simply check the boxes that reflect a source of tension for you and then use the lines below to elaborate more if necessary. Be completely honest with yourself or you won't get to the heart of your feelings. If you cannot be honest in this audit, you may as well put the book down and give up trying to move on with your life. Without being honest, you won't be able to come face to face with your weaknesses and then instigate the changes necessary over the long haul. Just as alcoholics can't succeed without first being brutally honest with themselves about their health, you won't be able to transform your life the way you envision unless you take a good hard look at your current situation, stop making excuses, and make the commitment to change. I recommend keeping this chart handy to refer back to because it informs so much of the book's message.

WHERE IS THE SOURCE OF TENSION IN YOUR LIFE?

Check as many of the following boxes to indicate where you are experiencing tension in your life, however big or small. Some tensions may entail multiple boxes, such as "spouse" and "money," or "spouse" and "parenting." Don't worry about linking different boxes, just focus on checking every box that resonates with you as a source of tension, even if it's related to another box. Then, in the *Why* column, jot down specifically why this is a source of tension or add any other details to help you identify with this tension more precisely. This can entail multiple reasons; for example, the strains in your relationship with your spouse may include issues about money, intimacy, and sharing parenting roles equally. Write as much down as you can. Remember, these are your private notes. No one has to see this. You may be surprised by what you discover as you think and write. I've offered an example of "why" in each category below.

CAREER   WHY?

❑ Job dissatisfaction _____

❑ Job loss _____ *I fear losing my job any day now.*

_____

❑ Future job potential _____

❑ Career direction _____

❑ Work projects _____

❑ Deadlines _____

❑ Expectations _____

❑ Education _____

FINANCIAL   WHY?

❑ Income _____

❑ Credit card debt _____

❑ Education loans _____

❑ Other debt _____

❑ Retirement plans _____

❑ Savings _____

❑ Spending habits/outflow _____

❑ Emergency fund _____

❑ Future financial needs _____

❑ Past financial mistakes _____

❑ Investments _____

❑ Mortgage   *I'm falling behind in my payments.*

_____

❑ Living expenses/bills _____

❑ Costs related to caring for others (e.g., parents, children) _____

_____

❑ Planning for the future _____

HEALTH   WHY?

❑ Overall health status _____

❑ Appearance   *I hate how I look. Old. Tired.*

_____

❑ Weight _____

❑ Fitness _____

❑ Chronic conditions / managing current health challenges ____

_____

❑ Stress load _____

❑ Psychological well-being _____

❑ Future health _____

PERSONAL   WHY?

❑ Time management
_____

❑ Household management
_____

❑ Personal upkeep / hygiene
_____

❑ Priorities / organization
_____

❑ Spirituality
_____

                                  I can't finish projects
❑ Goal setting / ability to get things done   *that I start.*

_____

❑ Making a difference in the world / giving back
_____

_____

❑ Emotional stability / happiness
_____

❑ Confidence / self-esteem
_____

❑ Sense of balance
_____

❑ Sense of personal fulfillment
_____

PEOPLE   WHY?

❑ Spouse / partner /
   girlfriend / boyfriend
_____

❑ Siblings

❑ Parents   *Need to talk to Dad about his health.*

❑ Children

❑ Extended family members

❑ Friends / neighbors

❑ Clients / boss

❑ Colleagues / co-workers

Take your time with this first phase of the personal audit. Really reflect on each of the above categories, and don't be afraid of what pops into your mind. My hope is that you begin to realize that you have strong sources of tension in areas of your life that you never realized before. Sometimes we may think that all of our issues are about money when other, equally straining, problems could exist that have nothing to do with our bank accounts or inability to pay bills. In fact, we may use financial difficulties as the *excuse* to avoid other personal challenges, such as a disconnect with our romantic partner, frustrations with colleagues at work or with our boss, and a dissatisfaction with our own shortcomings with regard to how we feel about our physical health and appearance.

In which category above did you check the most boxes? In which category are you strongest? Are your sources of tension mostly about other people or are they about you and the relationship you have with yourself? You may not necessarily be able to answer the "why" question to all of your sources of tension, and that's okay. There are no right or wrong answers here. I don't care if you checked every single box or every other box; this audit is simply a means to gauge your current well-being and psychological bearings—giving you the information you need to make beneficial changes.

Although this next phase of the personal audit will further help you to pinpoint tensions in your relationships specifically, don't move onward until you've devoted enough time and thought to this first phase to know what areas of your life need improvement. See if you can identify the top five sources of tension and write them down here:

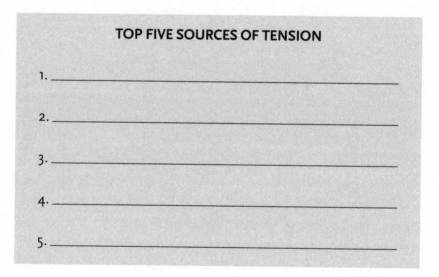

TOP FIVE SOURCES OF TENSION

1. _____

2. _____

3. _____

4. _____

5. _____

Note: Your top five sources of tension needn't come from each of the categories listed on the previous pages. They may all stem from the same category. But if you do find that the strains in your life are across the board, then go ahead and pick just one from each of the categories. Once you've determined your biggest sources of tension, it's time to move onward.

Personal Audit Phase II: Rate Your Relationships

Now, in the following table, rate how your relationships contribute to your life and your vision in these categories: financial, health, and personal development. Your personal vision entails the kinds of attitudes and values you want to have as well as the kind of person you want to be emotionally, psychologically, socially, and spiritually. You have to decide now whether a person, relationship, or feeling contributes to your personal development, or not. And if I haven't included enough lines, feel free to add any important people to this list.

HOW DO YOUR RELATIONSHIPS MEASURE UP TO YOUR VISION?

Rate the following relationships across three categories from 1 (no, they take away from my vision) to 5 (yes, they help me to live up to my vision every day).

FINANCIAL	HEALTH	PERSONAL
YOU and . . .		
Your partner:		
Your kids:		
Your parents:		
Your siblings:		
Your other family members:		

Your best friend: _____

Your boss: _____

Your co-workers: _____

Yourself: _____

Take a moment to look at what you've entered on the chart. What do these scores tell you about the people in your life? Are you surprised? What person or situation is not helping you create the life you want? Who supports and encourages you? Who is dragging you down?

As you examine and think about your responses, other questions to consider include: What role do these people play in your financial health, your physical health, and your spiritual health? Who sabotages your attempts to have a more balanced, happy life? When do any of these relationships ruin your sense of well-being and make you frustrated, insecure, or undermine your confidence? Which of these relationships brings you farther away from or closer to your overall vision? Do any of the people in your life demand more of your energy and time than you get to spend on yourself? Does anyone dampen your self-esteem or your ability to stay focused on your vision? How would you like these relationships to be different? Does a voice inside you cause trouble and encourage you to behave in ways you know you shouldn't? In other words, is the ongoing relationship with *yourself* actually a tremendous source of stress and internal discord?

When I met Cindy and Tom recently, they were the epitome of the young perfect newlywed couple just starting out. They acted lovey-dovey. They said they never fought. They didn't have much debt and were saving diligently for a down payment on a house. But as soon as I started asking some basic questions I could sense trouble. When

I asked them each questions about their values and thoughts on money (their "vision" for their financial life), their answers indicated that rather than being completely in sync their views were seriously divided. I knew that as soon as this couple had more access to credit and cash, they wouldn't be able to agree on what to spend it on or how to deal with debt. Tom was a fan of gadgets and the latest technology. Cindy, on the other hand, was an avid trader of stocks and socked away money each month (though she avoided contributing to her IRA account because that money wouldn't be accessible anytime soon). She wasn't so much into gadgets, but she was a lover of expensive restaurants and designer labels. They dined twice a week at fine restaurants, and once Cindy got pregnant they planned on her being a stay-at-home mom. I knew that if they continued to live the way they did, Tom's income alone would not suffice and too soon they'd be in debt up to their eyeballs.

It was also not a surprise for me to see that Cindy didn't like Tom's need for the latest and greatest gadget (but tolerated it since it didn't affect her bottom line—yet), and that Tom didn't care so much about fine meals and designer labels. If money ever got tight, though, what would go? What would be limited? How would they navigate their opposing values and differences in opinions? Dealing with money in good times might not be an issue but what about those times when things turn bad? Unless a couple is united, tough times can easily undo them. And that statement is the absolute truth when it comes to money issues.

So as you think about your financial situation, think about it in relation to others in your life who—like it or not—have an impact either directly or indirectly on your situation. It's very likely that the people and tensions in your life have a direct effect on your relationship with and attitude toward money. If you escape to a mall to avoid someone, or shop with friends to feel included, or buy things for your kids in attempts to gain compliance from them, then it's time to own up to this behavior. You cannot talk about your financial life in isolation. Even if you are single and have no children, money still comes into play with friends, co-workers, parents, siblings, and people you date.

Personal Audit Phase III: Assess How You Use Time

Although living on less is a forced reality for most people today, actually *doing* less is a luxury few of us can afford. We all feel that we are being asked to do more with less whether it's at work or at home. I've lost count of the times harried people say to me "If only there were more hours in the day" (there aren't!) and "If I only had more time" (you don't!). It seems that incredibly busy lives are a given. I don't know anyone who doesn't ache for the energy to meet the boundless demands of their day and the stamina to summit whatever new challenges they will face tomorrow. Every day it seems there's less time, less money, and even higher stakes in our lives. No wonder so few of us can get a good night's sleep and find time to rejuvenate while getting everything important done.

But maximizing your time is exactly what you must do as part of your newfound habits to take control of your life and reclaim your financial stability. You could be doing everything "right"— following your budget, cutting back on the things you really don't need, watching what you eat, staying active, and so on—but if you continue to drain your energy and your sense of well-being, what's the point? You're not getting to where you want to be fast enough. What gives?

The time we have in our lives, just like the space we have in our homes, is fixed. We can't magically get more time but we can manage the time we have more effectively. The word "manage" is interesting, it comes from the Latin word *manus* for hand. When we talk about managing our time or our lives, what we're really saying is that we're getting a hand (or a handle) on things. We have our "hands on the wheel." We're in charge and determining what direction things are taking. If you're not managing your time and your life, things very quickly get "out of hand" and chaos follows pretty soon thereafter. One of the major reasons people feel so drained and exhausted, tired and frustrated, is that they simply don't know how to manage the time they have. If this sounds like you I want you to stop and think for a moment. Where are your priorities? Do the things that you believe to be most important get the time they deserve? Are you on that list of things that don't get enough of your time? Is it impossible for you to find quality time for your partner or kids? Impossible to finish a project or get on top of your clutter? Is your life a giant avalanche of bigger and bigger balls you have to constantly juggle? When something comes across your desk, do you respond to it immediately no matter what? Is everything in your life "urgent" to the point that the urgent constantly takes precedence over what's truly important? If you're constantly in crisis mode then there is no way that you can feel in charge, in control, or in touch with yourself.

Use the following exercise to help you realize whether your time is well spent or a total waste.

ARE YOU IN A TIME WARP?

Which of the following sets of statements best relates to you? Choose one category that you most clearly identify with:

Category 1:
- I respond immediately to emails and phone calls 24/7. I don't have a system for letting some wait.
- I live with extreme energy highs and lows, and feel anxious all the time—I'm constantly in "crisis" mode.
- I say yes to everyone and everything, and am constantly putting out fires.
- I don't sleep well, have high blood pressure, and suffer from headaches and/or stomach problems.

- I don't make To-Do lists and have never been good with priorities.
- I pay bills at the last minute, or late.

If this sounds like you, you're **reactive** rather than proactive. Your money problems continue to accumulate and are a constant source of stress and strain (but you don't have time to deal with them).

Category 2:
- I love watching endless amounts of TV and surfing the internet. You can find me online late at night and emailing after I should have gone to bed.
- I love to shop without any goal in mind, even if it means I buy a lot of stuff I don't need.
- I have no idea what to expect of myself in the next year, in five years, or in ten years. I don't think about or plan for the future.
- From a physical standpoint, I've "let myself go."
- I pay bills when I feel like it, even if that means they are late.
- Stuff tends to pile up quickly at home, but I'm not motivated to clear it out.
- I feel emotionally empty and have a hard time meeting bigger, long-term goals for me and my family.

If this sounds like you, you're **inactive** and **indifferent**. Your money problems also continue to accumulate but you really don't care (and don't care to make time for them either). Your loved ones, on the other hand, worry about you a lot and get frustrated when their financial lives are impacted by your behavior.

Category 3:

- I'm a pretty good planner and map out my days carefully, including my meals, so that I get what I need to get done and eat well.
- I love setting goals for myself and planning out milestones to reach them. Mapping out my future, from tomorrow to years ahead, is something I take seriously.
- I don't let unimportant things distract me and I'm careful about creating boundaries when it comes to family time, and me time.
- I rarely feel deprived because I take responsibility for my choices and practice discipline.
- I share deep connections with others, feel energetic most of the time, and enjoy the thrill of learning something new.
- I pay my bills on time or early and have a system set up for taking care of my finances.

If this sounds like you, congratulations. You're **proactive** and life is probably pretty good. You don't have many problems with money, and the financial challenges that you do face are being carefully managed and cared for by you. Life for you is balanced and in order.

In which category did you find yourself? Are you mostly reactive (category 1), inactive (category 2), or proactive (category 3)? My guess is most of you fall into the reactive or inactive categories, though it's perfectly fine to see yourself with a mix of both. Chances are high that anyone who fits into category 1 or 2 has a cluttered financial and emotional life. It's virtually impossible to live in reactive or inactive mode without your finances and sense of well-being taking a hit. When you're reactive, you tend to spend without a clear plan, mindlessly and impulsively, and have no idea how to budget your money (or your time!). When you're inactive, your money problems fester and grow because they go unnoticed by you until you're forced to deal with them. At that point, your problems are so massive that you may continue to avoid facing them for as long as possible—meanwhile, you're driving everyone else in your life nuts!

In the next chapter I'll go into more details about how to take what you've learned about yourself from this time audit and do something positive with it. For now, just remember which category best describes you.

Dear Peter,
We decided that instead of things, we were going to have *experiences*. What we did is decide that all of our money goes directly into our accounts, and we keep a minute amount for daily things (fresh veggies from the store, a cup of coffee, etc.). All else is direct paid from the computer and we can see on a daily basis where our money is.

We soon discovered we didn't need so much stuff—and have made a concerted effort to get rid of a lot of what we had with recycling services, donations, etc. We also discovered our biggest enemies in this effort are the giant retailers and our walk-in closet! It was shameful what collected in there. So, we tore it out to use the space and put in a small wall closet. Impossible for it to become cluttered!

To get away with less, each time we want to purchase anything, we ask what *experience* can we gain instead. Will this small appliance buy tickets to a museum? Will this outfit buy a train fare to another city? Instead of buying this, can we have friends or family over for dinner? Generally speaking, we've answered "yes" to everything and now have a much fuller life. I've given up buying books and go to the library much more often.

In addition, I've also discovered how many free things are actually offered in the area. We share with friends and neighbors. For example, we like fondue. So one of us has the cheese set, the other the bullion set and we trade when needed. We do themed "pot lucks" where each guest brings a side dish and we have big dinners. Then we play board or card games after.

I think what this boils down to—no matter what reason you are trying to do without "things," it's about connecting with other people again.

CHASING HAPPINESS

The idea of happiness has gained a lot of attention in recent years, largely brought on by the scores of popular psychology books written to help people achieve more happiness. Of all the insights we've learned from recent studies, the most important is that happiness should be considered a process—not a goal. And another thing to keep in mind is that you have more control over your joy than you think.

Many things affect our happiness—our genes, our personal circumstances, and the choices that we make every day. We all know our circumstances can change quickly and though good changes, like buying a new car or getting a promotion, can make us feel happy in the beginning we quickly become accustomed to changed circumstances to the point that they no longer provide that same level of happiness. This explains why people, when asked to list what makes them happier, don't necessarily mention making more money, losing ten pounds, moving into a bigger house, or general success. Instead, when they are encouraged to really think hard about their sources of happiness, they talk in terms of their life's purpose, such as rearing smart, healthy children or bringing joy to others. When really pushed to define happiness, most people describe it as the sense of joy and fulfillment that comes from doing meaningful, worthwhile and engaging things that really affect their own or others' lives.

Earlier I asked you to think about where you derive your happiness. What gets you excited in a really big way? What do you value? What could you live without? What *can't* you live without? Let's return to that exercise and go a bit further. This time, I want you to consider not just your sources of happiness, but the things that get in the way of your happiness.

The Fire Drill: Imagine your house is on fire. You have only two minutes to vacate. Answer quickly:

The top three somethings I would make sure get out of the house in an extreme emergency are . . .

1. _____

2. _____

3. _____

My guess is you chose people and pets first, and then perhaps important documents and photographs, and a few heirlooms that hold sentimental value. Clearly, we all would pick our friends and family members as sources of happiness over things because our relationships, not our possessions, are what add depth and meaning to our lives. When we actually have to choose in such circumstances, we don't care that much about the high-ticket items like the television or state-of-the-art computer because those can be replaced and we know people can't.

Think again for a moment about what you'd grab from your home in a crisis and ask yourself the following:

I get most happiness from: _____

I am most happy when: _____

Your responses here are really worth thinking about. It's easy to get sidetracked by things and forget that they are not the source of lasting joy. So why do we spend so much of our time and energy on material things that, unlike the people in our lives, don't actually give us anything back?

Now let's take this one step further and explore the major hurdles between you and the happiness you deserve. Think about the items you'd take from your home in a crisis. What do these things tell you about what's important to you? Is there something that these things have in common? What is it about these items that you most value? If these items, and others like them, are the things that are most important to you, that bring you most happiness, think for a moment about all the other things you've surrounded yourself with. Is all that other "stuff" filling your life with happiness and joy? What is it about the items that you'd save that is missing from the other objects in your life that you still find so hard to let go? Consider these questions as you complete the following:

THE BIG THREE

Three things that get in the way of happiness in my life are:

1.  _____

2. _____

3. _____

If more than three impediments to your happiness come to mind, then list as many as you can.

When I do this exercise with people, among the many responses I hear are "my poor health," "my crappy relationship with my spouse," "my sick parent," "my debt," "my money problems," "my misery at work," "the way I look," "my problem teenager," "my lack of sleep," "my anxiety and unrelenting stress," "my chronic pain," and "my depression." This exercise always points to the big issues that people feel are holding them back from happiness—and most people's responses are rarely about possessions. When people really examine their lives, the lack of a flat-screen television is not really going to impede their happiness, nor will the luxury car missing from the garage.

The point of these exercises is to show you once again that happiness is about much more than what you own or the size of your home. Having things is not bad but our relentless quest for more can divert us from what's really important in our lives. At the same time it kills our happiness. When we fill our emotional holes with things that deepen our debt and take more open space away from us, we aren't doing anything helpful to feed and nurture ourselves. Quite the contrary, we're pushing true happiness farther away. When this pursuit of more becomes a way of avoiding deeper issues in our lives, the truth is we are actually making them worse and at the same time we could be creating additional problems like debt and clutter.

Dear Peter:
I have found my own way to live with less in these tough economic times. My husband and I budget our funds much more, eat out less, and plan "staycations" instead of traveling out of the area. I live outside of Washington, D.C. and there are so many wonderful museums, parks, and trails to visit

that I don't need to go more than thirty miles in any direction to see and/or do something new.

In terms of finding more inner peace and happiness, I begin each morning writing in my gratitude journal, listing the top five things that I am truly grateful for. This only takes one or two minutes, but it guarantees that the day begins in a uplifting and positive way. At the end of the day, I journal for about ten minutes to look back on the day and find the good things that occurred throughout the day as well.

Thank you for all that you do!

ON THE BRINK

Right about now you may feel like you're more overwhelmed than ever, because I've given you a lot to think about and take stock of in the last several rounds of exercises. Inhale and exhale deeply. Next up, I'm going to help you process all that information and emotion so it's a source of power and strength to effect the changes in your life that were the reason you picked up this book.

4

Create Space for What Really Matters

LAST YEAR, WHILE FLYING ACROSS THE COUNTRY, I struck up a conversation with a fellow passenger who reminded me again that it's never about the stuff. We started with the usual pleasantries typical of a first encounter, and early on I detected a deep sadness in this woman. She said she had just been visiting family for Thanksgiving and that it had been a long time since she'd traveled so far. I'll admit, sometimes when I tell people what I do for a living, they wonder what satisfaction I could possibly get out of helping strangers declutter their homes and deal with all of that, well, junk. I quickly remind these people that for me it's not so much about decluttering homes as it is about decluttering entire lives. For me, it's all about helping people reframe their relationship to what they own so that the focus is no longer on the quantity of stuff but on the quality of their relationships.

The woman on the airplane, whom I'll call Elly, recognized me from a segment I had done on the *Oprah Winfrey* show and tearfully asked me for help. Elly seemed very put together but quickly, as she shared with me the details of her recent life, I realized that looks could be deceiving. As she talked, I felt as though I were the first person she trusted to open up to about her problems and sorrows. I sat there listening, knowing the best thing I could do for her now was just to sit and hear her story.

Elly had suffered two devastating losses that year. Two weeks after she celebrated her first-born son's wedding high on a hilltop outside San Diego, her newlywed son was killed in a freak car accident. No more than a month after that, her husband of forty years was diagnosed with terminal cancer and lived for just three months. For the first time in her adult life, Elly was alone, though she still had two other grown children. Elly explained that she barely recognized herself anymore. She'd gained nearly forty pounds in the past six months, had "let herself go," and her home was "rotting." She wouldn't let her other children help her, and they lived far enough away they couldn't see how she was living or how far she had slipped from her "previous life." It had been eight months since she'd buried her husband, and Elly had pretty much withdrawn from society during that time in order to deal with her pain.

I scheduled a visit with Elly that very next day. She happened to live only about thirty miles from me in Los Angeles. From the outside of her house, where she had lived for nearly as long as she'd been married, I could tell that this had been a home of homes. It was the place she had raised her children and nursed her late husband through his final days. It was where all of her life's memories clung to every nook and cranny.

But this wasn't a happy home anymore, at least from what I could see when I arrived. It had become overrun by stuff—stuff that reflected Elly's recent losses and pain. Clearly, the dual tragedies had paralyzed her and she was living in inactive mode. While taking me on a house tour, Elly spoke in terms of "before" and "after," telling me she'd been an avid house cleaner and stoic shopper who previously never let clutter invade her space. She had been good with money and had worn the CEO hat in the family for decades. I believed all this to be true but it was hard to imagine those days when looking at the state of her house. Now she couldn't find that industrious manager's hat to save herself. She'd let bills go unpaid because she couldn't face the paperwork. Her savings had been used up from paying the medical bills and funeral costs, and because her husband had been the breadwinner she had no income outside of social security and his insurance policy. Elly still didn't have a job, nor did she seem to have the inclination to look for one. Part of her was still trying to live as though her circumstances had not changed but part of her was no longer functioning. Unanswered mail had piled up and the kitchen looked as though someone had been camping out for months. She had turned one of the bedrooms into a shrine dedicated to her late son. Her husband's clothes still filled the closets, his toiletries were strewn across the bathroom sink and bedroom vanity. Elly hadn't been able to move or touch anything for fear of losing the memories. Until now, that is. After she gave me a tour of her home, she turned to me and said, "I'm ready, Peter. I really am." I held her hands in reassurance. I knew she was finally ready to create space for what really mattered.

READY FOR CHANGE

Though you may not see yourself in Elly or think your life is nearly as "bad" as hers, I bet you'd be able to find plenty of similarities if you looked closer. In most of the people I work with, there's a common theme: a sense of loss (for whatever reason) and an inability to take charge of one's life. You may not be mourning the loss of family members, but dealing with the loss of a lifestyle you once lived can be plenty to shoulder. Letting bills pile up, avoiding the personal and physical upkeep you should be doing in your life, and letting yourself go are all challenges that I see routinely in people. And the solution for each and every one of them—regardless of personal issues and circumstances—is usually the same: taking slow, methodical steps to reclaim a healthy, organized, and financially and emotionally fit life again.

Elly's readiness for change was the first critical step in actually making changes. She committed to and embraced the need for change. This will also be your first important step. Until we are ready, we can hear the message, but never accept it as real so we never change. This happens all the time in the diet world. Resources and advice on weight loss abound, but we still suffer from obesity. Anyone who has ever lost a significant amount of weight and kept it off has succeeded in one simple thing: redefining his or her relationship with food. The same holds true in terms of our possessions or money. Once you redefine your relationship to what you own and how you spend money, you can make a lasting, permanent shift in your life. If there's not a personal desire for change, however, there's no point even getting started. The desire for something different, something better, has to first come from within yourself.

If you've gotten this far in the book, you have to ask yourself whether or not you are ready to make changes. These changes will mean dealing with all the emotions that are tied up in your relationships, your physical stuff, your financial hardships, and so on. Getting organized for the sake of getting organized is a waste of time. So is cleaning up your garage to make room for an old piece of furniture you now have to store because you just bought a new one for the living room. Paying a single bill just to get rid of it is beside the point. And so is creating an elaborate filing system and an organized space to pay bills that you never routinely use. Taking charge of any single area in your life should lead to much bigger, loftier goals. It should also affect more than just that one area you're trying to clean up. The various aspects of our lives—emotional, financial, physical, and so on—are all interrelated. If we fix how we organize our home, we have to fix how we handle money and finances. If we address our feelings and sources of tension, we have to address what we think about our possessions and how we value what we choose to buy and maintain. Though we may set specific, targeted goals for any one area of our life, each goal should ultimately help us live a richer, less stressed, more happy and focused life. Now, those are goals worth pursuing!

As you're no doubt beginning to do as you read, I took Elly through the process of understanding why she'd let her life go so awry. Often with a life overwhelmed by clutter there is some trauma that has precipitated it all, some event that throws you and your life off track and Elly was no different. Clearly, the emotional impact of her losses had been monumental enough to derail her life. When such a trauma hits, the stuff you own can become a way of insulating yourself from the pain and the overwhelming confusion of dealing with each day. What losses or traumas have affected you? Can you see a connection between certain circumstances in your life and how you've lost control of that life along the way? Do you harbor a hidden sadness or aggression that has changed how you'd like to live?

As with so many of the people I deal with, I first gave Elly permission to accept how she had chosen to grieve. This may sound odd but often people look to me for some permission that they are not able to give themselves—the permission to let go, the permission to move on, the permission to say no, or just the permission to accept that they are worthy of a better life. I also encouraged Elly to reframe how she could celebrate her husband and son in a way that gave her back her life and yet also honored and respected their memory. She knew it was time to pick herself up and find a new normal. She just couldn't do it herself. Although I was a stranger to her, I was a neutral third party who could intervene on her behalf and help her to take stock of her things, her emotions, and her life in a way she knew she could not.

At the end of the first day working with Elly, I was amazed by the light that came back into her eyes. She looked as if she'd just been liberated from a prison. Though her grief was still very present and real, she could separate her emotions from the things and put those things in their proper place. It's always amazing to see what happens when you remove clutter from someone's life. I've said it often but it's hard to imagine what great things flow into a space once the clutter is removed. This was so true for Elly—more space, more light, a more optimistic outlook had increased her hope for the future, and given her a sense of peace and calm and, perhaps most important, a sense that she had her life back. It wouldn't be the same life, but it would be a life she could enjoy. Elly even began to contemplate jobs she could apply for, hoping to secure a regular flow of income once again.

Together we also tackled her stacks of bills and reorganized her bill-paying system. For Elly, writing a check to pay that first overdue bill was all she needed to get going again in that department. It was like the law of inertia. She'd been stuck for a long time, and simply needed a little push to get her back on track. Again, this is not unusual. No matter what form the clutter takes, it's often about just getting started, about seeing that you can turn things around. I reminded Elly that getting back on track was not only doing something for herself but would ultimately enable her to live the best life that she could, preserving her family's legacy and honoring those closest to her who had passed away.

My hope is that you, too, can turn your life around using the same step-by-step methods I used with Elly. You've already begun the process and now it's just a matter of continuing onward with your own determination and a fearless attitude.

Dear Peter:
I will be turning fifty-five in May, and I have finally found my freedom in having less. But in having less, I am learning to buy what I use and use what I buy. Rather than having a pantry, cabinet, or closet full of items that I don't ever use, I now have only items that I need . . . with more space in those

places. As I'm working my way through our home, it's making me feel less cluttered.

I'm not 100 percent there, but 85 percent. My father died a couple of years back. We had to sell the home, and now my mom rotates between our home and that of two of my siblings. We have divided up their sixty-one years of "stuff." As I look at the things my dad decided to move around for his entire adult life, I hear you saying, "If it's so valuable, why has it rotted in a box, or why do you have it in a box." Thanks for your help over the years in the shows you've been on, giving me the equipment to face "things."

YOUR PERSONAL LIFE IS MULTIDIMENSIONAL

It doesn't take a serious loss or tragedy to make someone spiral down into clutter and debt. Nor does it take reaching the proverbial depths of that catastrophe to stop and hear the wake-up call. In fact, maybe you cannot pin your current state of affairs on a single event or loss in the past. Life is multidimensional, a web of intricate experiences and feelings that can shine one color today and a different color tomorrow. Where you stand today could be the culmination of several events and circumstances that have piled up over the years.

Take a look at your personal inventory now. Where do you see the tension in your life? Is it really in your physical stuff and debt? Or is it crouching somewhere else, manifesting itself in your clutter and debt? My guess would be the latter. Just like clutter and debt, which sneak up on you until they overwhelm you, tension is deceptive. Take a hard look at your situation and make an honest assessment of the sources of tension in your life. You may be frustrated at work, but is the tension really between you and our spouse? You may be angered by your children's recent behavior, but is the tension really between you and your weight? You may think the tension in your life stems from your unpaid student loans, but is it really coming from the fact that you haven't figured out what you want to do with your life and you hate your current job? Be honest. Here is an opportunity to own up to what's really happening in your home and your life. Here is a chance to build on that honesty in a way that touches all areas of your life.

Take the time to really focus on interpreting your personal audit honestly. Below are some helpful questions and guidelines to assess further different categories that can affect your 360-degree view.

Relationships: Who's Helping, Who's Hurting?

Recall that I had you rank how different people in your life either were contributing or taking away from the vision you have for yourself in the areas of your finances, health, and personal development.

Take a moment and reflect again on your personal audit from the last chapter, especially Phase II starting on page 69, which specifically had you reflect on your relationships. List three things from that exercise that surprised you or that were revelations to you:

1. _____

2. _____

3. _____

What caught you off guard? What did you find that you didn't expect, or that you did but may never have owned up to fully? Did you peg someone as hurting your vision that you never expected? What will you do about it? Does that revelation motivate you or utterly scare you? How will you move forward with this new information about your relationships? For how long will you allow those who trample on your vision to control what you want from your life?

I can't stress enough the power of ongoing communication with your loved ones and the people with whom you share space and money—and emotions. As I've been saying all along, our relationships lie at the core of our being and often dictate how we behave— how we buy, how we save money, how we plan our futures, and even how we perceive ourselves. Because of this, when our relationships are not in harmony with how we want to live, everything else in our lives is out of balance. No wonder the common phrase "I need some space" creeps into our vehement conversations when we're at odds with a loved one. Physical space, mental space, and emotional space are really all the same thing. I've said this so many times—our homes, our heads, our hearts, and our hips are all connected. Maybe it's time to tweak that list by saying that our homes, our heads, our hearts, and our hip pockets are all connected. Touch one, you touch them all!

I'm no longer surprised when I hear about couples who finally deal with their clutter and debt, and in the process end their relationship. For some people, once they face the fear that motivated them to hold onto useless things and let the bills pile up, they come face to face with the previously hidden problems in their relationship. And as they get over the fear of dealing with their stuff and debt, they also get over the fear of dealing with their relationship. Clutter and debt will never preserve a healthy partnership, and their removal won't destroy a fulfilling one.

Being silent about your feelings, vision, and financial reality is not protecting your family; it's actually exposing them to bigger problems. And not dealing openly with your situation is the same as saying "I don't trust you enough to deal with this together." If a relationship is not based on honesty, then how solid can it be? The only couples who break up in the face of a clean, organized, and financially fit home are the ones who realize how much more they want and deserve from life.

The good news is this also works the other way. Couples who have been bogged down by their clutter and debt may experience a revitalization of romance when their space and bills are cleared, and once they are sharing a vision as a team. The great thing about decluttering and getting financially in shape is that this cannot be done without real communication. Very quickly couples find themselves talking openly about what they value, what they fear, how they see themselves as a couple in the future, and what is important to them. For those whose relationship is based on what they own, or whose only sense of unity comes from the clutter and buying more together regardless of the ability to pay, this process can be difficult and heartbreaking. But if your relationship has a strong base, the process of rethinking the function of your home and your relationship to your belongings and money inevitably strengthens what you have and who you are.

Part of imagining your ideal life is envisioning the relationships you want—the companionship, the support, the love. If your relationships are full of emotional clutter, now is the time to clear it away and to look honestly at how you want to cultivate your relationships in the future.

WHICH EXCUSES DO YOU LIVE BY?

When I suggest that couples start talking to each other, I often hear: *But I don't know how to talk about this with my partner—it'll start a fight.* There are lots of excuses that get in the way of people's ability to move forward, and this is often a big one. Similarly, when you took your personal audit, you may have noticed a little voice inside your head saying "But it's not my fault!" or "I don't have the time no matter how hard I try!" Don't be ashamed if you did. That reaction is completely human but we have to deal with it.

In fact, we have to deal with all of your excuses. So, starting here and sprinkled throughout the upcoming pages I'm going to cover the most common excuses I hear and give you the ammo to knock them down one by one. In doing so, I'll share with you how these excuses are holding you back from your vision, and what you can do about them today.

Excuse #1: I Can't Talk about This with My Partner—I'll Start a Fight

If I had a dollar for every time I heard this excuse, I'd be rich. Chalk it up to another unfortunate aspect of our human nature: tough talk is, well, tough! Who likes to start difficult and emotionally trying conversations? Who enjoys openly discussing their shortfalls and failures? Everyone is scared of starting a fight or upsetting someone. But everyone knows deep down that honesty is a requirement in any fulfilling relationship.

What makes starting these conversations so tough is that the established roles in a relationship can be a roadblock to open communication. For example, if the man typically acts as the head-of-household but the woman is trying to take the lead and instigate this conversation about money, values, goals, the family's spending, and so on, the balance of power can be thrown off. Divided roles can get in the way of talking honestly about difficult subjects; the woman may end up kowtowing to her husband rather than taking charge for the benefit of the whole family. Many men also feel the need to "protect" their partners and families from bad news. Admitting to financial troubles can be threatening to a man because it implies that he is not a good provider or taking care of his family properly.

The other challenge to this conversation is that it calls for a change in habits. And we all know that ingrained habits are hard to break. If your family has been living large for years, living on less can seem unappealing at first. Not buying whatever you want whenever you want it may feel like you're seriously depriving yourself and your family of things you've come to believe you all deserve. This is why these conversations are absolutely essential. If you're not openly exchanging ideas and feelings about the things that are important to you, how can you find compromise and agree on a plan that everyone can live with and be happy with as you pursue much larger goals in life?

The Financial Impact: You'll Dig Yourself Deeper

If you're in a committed relationship, I am guessing that you're in it for the long haul—for better or for worse. A shared life means shared responsibilities and if one of you is carrying the financial burden, or you're both living in fear of having an honest discussion about money, then you can never hope to create any kind of honest and secure life together—let alone a secure financial life. Spending will become an escape from reality and by the time circumstances force you to face financial facts, chances are it'll be too late to reverse the damage.

The Solution: Get Talking, Starting with Love

Stop putting off the inevitable. You know you need to speak up and take the lead in broaching the subject of money with your partner. The goal is to do this gently with a lot of love and steer clear of going into attack mode. If it helps, practice how you'll start the conversation and have a plan for when you'll do it. I've given you a sample script to use that can help you with that very first and terrifying sentence. Whether you go unscripted or choose to write down exactly what you want to say, be sure to incorporate frequent statements about how much you love and care for this person, especially if the conversation starts to get heated. Remember, you're doing this for both of you.

What You Need to Do Today

Tonight sit down with your partner. No disruptions. No TV. No kids. Use the script in the box to start the conversation. It may not all happen in one sitting but use this conversation to identify areas for growth and change, and start to create your shared action plan for making the necessary changes happen (the exercises throughout this book will help you do this). Regularly check in with each other and reaffirm your love and support for each other. Share responsibility for how you got into this situation and for the action plan that will help you get out of it. Keep each other informed and accountable.

LET'S GET THE CONVERSATION STARTED!
THE PARTNER SCRIPT

Money and emotions got your tongue? Use the following script to break the ice and initiate a conversation with your partner. Make sure to start this conversation in a comfortable setting and away from major distractions (no phones, television, children, computers, etc.). Find a time when it's convenient for both of you to be focused and attentive to each other. You may find that your first conversation winds up being about scheduling a time later on when you can have the full conversation. That's okay, don't get frustrated. The extra time will help both of you pull your thoughts together.

Say to your partner: "I have something really important that I want to talk with you about and I'm frightened to open up this discussion. But because I love you and want to spend my life with you, I think it's something we have to talk about now."

Then introduce some of the fears and concerns you have about your financial life. Let the tears flow if they surface. Have some tissues nearby.

Stay focused on the issue. Avoid personal attacks or cheap shots. If you find yourself saying "you, you, you" a lot, try to use more "I" or "we" instead and notice how that changes how you feel about what you are saying.

If things start to get heated, remind your partner that you are in this together and you both want to get out from under the stress that's causing problems for both of you and for your relationship.

Talk the issue through. You may not resolve everything in one sitting but you've started the conversation and that's a great thing.

Before you end the conversation agree on a time when

you can continue the discussion and then make a firm date. (If you don't make a date and write it into your calendars it won't happen.) Decide on what you'll both do *now* to address the issues that have been raised and what issues you need to cover next time. Talk, plan, revisit—it's a healthy cycle to get into!

Dear Peter:

Our family went into this economic downturn in a not-so-good place. I believe in America we are wasteful and expect so much in our lives. We have always been in the lower middle class and have not had what others do, but we would still want things we didn't really need. Now we have a lot of stuff that we really don't use and need to clear out. We only have about 1,200 square feet of living space for four people, so it will do us good to declutter our lives. We are just starting and have a long way to go. We are definitely much more conscious about what we are doing and for the first time have an emergency fund and have not used a credit card in a year now. We are embracing the thought of having more control in our lives and enjoying just spending time together and learning more about things together. I think it would be a wonderful thing for more of us to decide to live with less and think about what we are doing. The world isn't going to get better until we do.

We have to take responsibility and it all starts at home.

Excuse #2: Time—There Just Isn't Any!

When you checked the pulse of how you use your time on page 73, which category did you find yourself under? Are you someone who lives in reactive mode, someone who is largely inactive, or do you really work at being proactive and plan your life accordingly? If you've got money issues, then I doubt you're living a proactive life today. Anyone who feels constantly time crunched and living under the weight of too much to do and no time to do it is likely money crunched as well, and living under the weight of too much debt. The two go hand in hand.

If you're still fretting over whether you're "reactive" or "inactive," don't! You may be a mixture of both—living in reactive mode when it comes to things like checking unnecessary email obsessively but being inactive when it comes to checking important bills and responding to them promptly. Hybrids of reactive and inactive people are everywhere and they generally are challenged by the task of prioritizing and creating realistic To-Do lists—not just for their daily lives but for what they need to achieve their true vision as well. The solution? Develop a system for organizing your life according to what needs to get done now, what can wait until later, and what can hold off for *much* later. Use this system for everything during your day that demands for your attention, whether it be a phone call, an unhappy child, or a piece of mail. Prioritize your tasks by creating To-Dos marked "now," "later," and "can wait." Set standards for dealing with important monthly stuff like bills, such as designating every other Sunday each month to address the unpaid bills or mail that requires your attention.

If you're the reactive type who's easily distracted by email, incoming calls on your cell phone, or the television, then you may want to create boundaries for yourself whereby you only check email, watch television, or have your cell phone turned on during certain hours of the day. You may choose to create this time for yourself early in the morning before kids and school and work distract you. Or maybe you are better in the evening when everything has quieted down again before bedtime.

If you're the inactive type who can be pulled into the mindless vortex of TV watching, internet surfing, game playing, or any other time zappers that let you put off what you need to be doing, avoid turning on the TV or computer during the hours you've dedicated for getting things done. Use the designated productive time to complete the tasks that should be dealt with as soon as possible, or that require routine maintenance such as tidying up your living quarters and balancing your checkbook.

I don't care who you are. Whether you're working three jobs or living a life of leisure, there's never enough time to finish all the To-Dos. We all have lists of things to do that exceed the physical limitations of our time and energy, and the last thing you want to do is use your precious "free time" to clean out your clutter and get things in order. Every moment of time you devote to getting on top of your stuff you don't get to spend accomplishing something else, something you might think is more important.

But here's another way to look at it. You say you don't have time, but considering that clutter *monopolizes* our time, and prevents us from *capitalizing* on our time, imagine all the time you'll magically *create* by just getting this one area in your life under control? If you stop and add up how many minutes each week you spend hunting for your keys, talking to another creditor to avoid a late payment, or looking for a piece of paper that contains information you need to give to your daughter for school, you'll find you have a significant amount of "lost time" that could have been better spent doing something to help you make real the vision you have for the life you want. The time you lose because of the clutter is time you will never get back. Throwing your time away is as bad as throwing your money away on buying that clutter in the first place! One effect of clutter is that you shut down. Instead of actively living your life you wind up stressed, giving all your energy and time to the clutter rather than to the things that really matter to you. No matter how far behind you are, you have to make the time to free yourself from clutter. When you remember that clutter costs time *and* money you'll realize that getting rid of the clutter is truly an investment in yourself. After you've made that investment and changed the order of your home, you'll see that the time you invested will come back to you with interest.

> Dear Peter:
> I have joined a ladies gym, which sounds like I have just spent more money, but it has actually done the opposite. I absolutely love going, have lost inches from across my body and lost pounds, too. I am finding that exercising is saving me a fortune, as I spend most of my spare time at the gym, I no longer go to the shopping centre and spend my money on all of those unnecessary items (clutter) and no longer buy junk food. Being healthy is an awesome way to save money, my life is much happier now that I have less! Less clutter and less of me, I couldn't ask for more!

The Financial Impact: You Live Constantly Feeling Out of Control, and So Do Your Finances

When you feel that your time is not your own, or that you're constantly time challenged, you can very quickly feel out of control. This results in poor decision making, last-minute and ill-thought-out purchases, no planning, and a constant sense of stress created by always running behind.

The Solution: Get Your Priorities Straight

Give time to what you believe to be important. The best investment you can make is in your own life.

What You Need to Do Today

Look where you're spending your time and what that means about what you believe (whether you admit it or not) to be important in your life. Note that you may use time differently at work than you do at home. Where are you more efficient? Most of us tend to be a little more organized at work than we are at home, but we can squander just as much time in each setting that could otherwise be used to get more accomplished. All of the ideas here will help you to gain control of your time in every setting that you find yourself in.

- Get control of your paperwork by creating a mail center. Your mail center will be the place where all mail goes and gets dealt with. If you can, you should have a shredder here for immediately discarding unwanted mail that contains personal information, such as credit card invitations and coupons that have been personalized with your name. If you don't own a shredder, don't go buy one. Ripping the mail up works fine, too. Just make sure you stay on top of it and go through your mail once a day so it doesn't build up and you don't lose anything.
- Structure your own day and take control of every minute. Don't let incoming work control you. Phone calls and email can arrive sounding urgent and demanding immediate attention. Don't let them divert your focus. Trust yourself to decide what gets priority.
- Get your email under control. These days email is a critical part of our lives, whether at home or at work. But some of it can be distracting and the frequency with which you check email can mean the difference between getting stuff done and feeling scattered and unaccomplished. Regardless of your situation, you can take measures to handle your email with maximum efficiency. Tackle your email in batches at certain times of the day (when *you* decide rather than when you hear that "ping" of an incoming message). Controlling email will have an immediate impact on your productivity and effectiveness.
- Establish boundaries. Set specific time periods during which certain tasks get completed while other, less important tasks can wait. If you're prone to distractions, have a system in place for block-

ing out these intrusions and addressing them only during certain times of the day.

- It bears repeating: don't let the urgent take precedence over the important. It's easy to let emergencies or the latest crisis run your day. If you don't develop the skill of separating the urgent from the important you won't ever feel in control. Identify those tasks that most need your attention and don't allow yourself to be easily or unnecessarily distracted. Just because someone puts one of those High Priority flags on their email doesn't automatically make it so. Prioritize. Prioritize. Prioritize and manage your day accordingly.
- Adopt a calendar system. Use either your computer or a paper calendar to plan your days, weeks, and life ahead.
- Get some control by setting up a message center in your home. Hang a calendar and list important dates. Hang a white board to jot down important lists, To-Dos, or that thought you don't want to lose. Try a cork board, too, to pin those circulars, notices, or invitations that you don't want to forget.
- Assign a specific day of the week for chores and get everyone involved by dividing up responsibilities. Set a time and day for laundry, food shopping, meal planning, house clean up, and so on.
- Pay your bills at the same time on the same day every week or every other week. And monitor your account online wherever you can.

Everyone wants more time, and the good news is that more time is there waiting for you if you just learn how to better manage your time. A stronger financial life is also waiting for you if you just learn to manage your attitudes and your money better. Being the perfect manager in these departments won't happen overnight, but the tools you're gaining in this book will help you to take the steps in the right direction. Just knowing whether or not you're the type to be in reactive or inactive mode is helpful in making the conscious choice to become a proactive individual.

The benefits of managing your time better work the kind of magic that following a routine exercise program can have. Like exercise, optimal time management will spill into every aspect of your life. You'll have more time to do the things you really want to do (and the truly unimportant, yet mentally exhausting stuff will melt away). You'll feel less stressed out and may even experience a transformation in your health as a result. You'll become a wizard at knowing the difference between "urgent" and "can wait" and saying "No" to unnecessary things that sap your energy and don't add to your life. You'll be motivated to face your finances and keep up with managing your financial life even when times are tough or money is tight. And you'll find plenty of extra time for *you* time—for engaging in the activities that satisfy your soul and raise the quality of your life.

People who are masters at time management are masters in most areas of their lives. Why? Because just about everything we do shares time as a common denominator. Time is the engine of our day. If you can master time, you can master just about anything.

Note: Parenting and Protecting Your Children— Are You Helping or Hurting Their Future?

Contrary to popular wisdom, adults haven't been the only victims of the recession. Children have become hidden casualties, often absorbing more than their parents are fully aware of. Several academic studies have linked parental job loss—especially that of fathers—to adverse impacts in areas like school performance and self-esteem. A variety of studies have tied drops in family income to negative effects on children's development. A recent study at the University of California, Davis, found that children in families where the head of the household had lost a job were 15 percent more likely to repeat a grade. That's significant! Other studies have confirmed similar findings, many of them also showing how a child's emotional well-being declines when a family endures unemployment. In the long term, studies have shown that children whose parents were laid off have been found to have lower annual earnings as adults than those whose parents remained employed. What's more, according to the

American Psychological Association, 30 percent of kids between eight and seventeen years old worry about money.

I've witnessed this cause and effect on a variety of levels among the families who have been living on the brink. Parents who suffered job loss and such drastic income reduction that it's become difficult to put food on the table have shared with me how they've watched their children's behavior take a nosedive and their stress levels increase. This in turn has a negative impact on the parents' marriage, adding another stressor to what could already be a shaky relationship. I can't tell you how many times I've seen couples working so hard to help their children and at the same time are struggling to save their marriage. The stress of keeping all the balls in the air—the unhappy children, the job instability, the income decline, the debt, the clutter and disarray at home—is intense. Sometimes it's too intense for the most loving relationship to handle.

But you don't need to be living on the brink or experiencing rock bottom yourself to see a shift in your children's behavior during financially strapped times. Children can pick up signals that increase their own stress from just about everywhere now—their friends, their friends' parents, the media, your bad day at work, or the argument you had last night with your spouse about paying for summer camp. Children are not immune to the pressures of modern life and we frequently underestimate their ability to pick up on what is actually happening in their adult-driven world. If you and your spouse constantly bicker about money, what effect does this have on your kids? Do they retreat to a closet or bathroom to complete homework assignments because that's the only place they can hear themselves think? Does the topic of money scare them because they know how much it scares you? If you and your partner are fighting about money, how do you think that affects your children's concept of money?

Changes in family dynamics are inevitable, whether we're going through good times or bad. Adaptability has been key to human survival, and it is the key to your family's survival, too. This is why I continue to emphasize the value of including your children in all family conversations even—or especially—when the conversation is about money. Family meetings shouldn't be an annual event and they should involve your children—even when you are dealing with tough or messy decisions. Showing your kids that you value and are interested in their ideas and opinions helps them understand that they play an important and valuable part in your family's life. Fear comes from the unknown. You can reduce that fear for your children by involving them in decision making, by explaining your plans and by showing them that you are in control of the forces that affect your family every day. Most of all, and you may need to learn this first yourself: teach them that money should be viewed as a source of knowledge, education, freedom, and independence—not the monster bill collector who calls every night during dinner.

In addition to being affected by the financial climate, your kids are influenced by the state of their physical space. Don't for a minute think that your children are not dramatically affected by clutter and disorganization just as you are. Behavioral problems and learning difficulties often emerge when kids are wildly overstimulated in their clutter-filled homes. Your children will not easily or openly admit to clutter or emotional chaos being a problem but it will eat away at them on a subconscious level and eventually they will show their pain through their actions.

When your home is overrun with clutter and debt, you're channeling a hopeless message of *I don't like this, but I can't change it* into your children. Or worse, *money is bad and debt is inevitable.* They learn to push away their emotions like you and absorb a message of powerlessness. This learned helplessness is one of the most insidious aspects of clutter and debt that parents almost always fail to realize or acknowledge. Its impact on kids is tremendous. If fear and denial are strong emotions in your home they will definitely affect your children. You have to get a grip on these emotions so they don't grip your children. They can't adopt money-savvy habits without your lead. You teach by example. What example are you teaching today?

Get Your Family on Board ASAP!

I've dedicated a lot of chapter 8 to the essentials of bringing your family together and including them—and their reluctance and frustrations—into your overall vision. Once you've brought your spouse or partner into the conversation, inviting your children into the discussion is critical.

Don't wait until it's too late to teach your children social responsibility, manners, decision-making skills, personal accountability, debt and credit management (even before they can apply for credit!), respect for property, and tolerance of others. All of these fundamental human values are taught from the moment a child becomes aware of his or her surroundings. Create order, establish limits, encourage routines, and foster organization in your home to model the behavior and values you want your children to adopt.

Excuse #3: I Don't Know How It Got So Bad

One thing that constantly surprises me is that regardless of the amount of clutter in a person's life—from financial to emotional and physical—people often express some surprise at it being there, as if they woke up one day and suddenly realized that they were far from where they wanted to be. "I don't know how my life got like this!" is what I hear. People freely admit that it's their life (no once forced them to make the decisions they have made), but in the next breath they tell me they are confounded by how it all got so bad. Just when did things go awry? What triggered the downfall? Why didn't I see it? How did this happen? It sounds like they're trying to place blame on anyone and anything but themselves. They are so busy living that they don't take the time to stop and reflect on their life, whether it's the stuff they own, the relationships they have, or the way they spend their time, energy, and money. So it's easy to suddenly find their lives full of things that they don't really need, use, or want—be it their closets, their commitments, friends, job, or daily responsibilities. This leaves many feeling out of control and unable to accept responsibility.

It's important to take full responsibility for your life, to do whatever you can to get back into the driver's seat, and to change the things you don't like. Your life is your own—it's what you've created. The stuff that fills your home is yours, the debt that fills your bank statements was created by you, and the unhappiness and dissatisfaction that pervades your days is within you and has been growing for some time. While it's important to own your life and your choices, you shouldn't feel like the magnitude of your problems gives you permission to just give up. Wishing things away won't make them disappear but working together with a plan for your better future will definitely help.

The Financial Impact: You Fail to Successfully Deal with Your Debt

You are responsible for your life and no one will create the life you want except you. If you constantly avoid dealing with the factors that got your life this way, because nothing is ever your fault, then your finances and your life will never be stable. Shrugging your shoulders and expressing doubt or indifference to your problems will only make them bigger. Until you own up to your problems and face them head on, you'll continue to fall deeper into debt and endure an endless assault of consequences.

The Solution: Own Up, 'Fess Up, and Take Responsibility

I know that this is very tough talk, but here's the bottom line: you have to stop acting like a victim. You've played that part exceptionally well up to now, but it's time to take on a different role. Don't waste any more precious time being irresponsible. To say that you don't know how it got so bad is just another way of saying, "I'm helpless in the face of my problems," or "my problems own me." This way of thinking and behaving might have worked when you were little and someone had to take care of you, but now you're an adult and no one is going to rescue you or give you what you need except you. Change comes with action, and now is the time for long-term positive change!

What You Need to Do Today

Look clearly at where you are in your life and say to yourself, "This is my life. Only I am able to make the changes necessary to deal with my problems. I am responsible for my life and my actions. Nothing has control over me but me. Not anyone else, not my stuff, not my debt, not my self-doubt, and certainly not my fear of taking control."

Excuse #4: But It's Not My Fault

You know what I'm going to say about this one. Ahem, see previous excuse about not taking responsibility and owning up to your quagmire. Maybe you think it should be your partner or children who should be reading this book, and yes, they should—and will—be part of this whole process. But no matter how many people contribute to your life and your problems, you have to take a personal stand all on your own. Everyone with whom you share money, time, space, and emotions will be part of your solution but regardless of their contribution, you alone must accept full responsibility. For everything. Seriously.

If you don't believe you have a problem (because it's not your fault!) and someone has given this book to you, listen up. If you and your partner are not on the same page, your relationship has to be suffering. I see it all the time among couples who have different views of how to live with regard to money and space. One partner will have no problem harboring dozens of partially filled or empty boxes in a basement or garage (just in case they move or need to store "important things") while the other just wants to throw everything away and turn that unused space into a useful room for the family. One person will be the spender and the other will be the saver. Your goal, then, is to meet on common ground somewhere and find a reasonable compromise that keeps your relationship strong and your vision alive.

Dear Peter:

Living by less is a dream I would love to achieve. I think and feel that we as a family are living above our means. I know that it is beginning to become a problem. Because of our actions our children are spoiled, we are spoiled, and we are greatly in debt. Living paycheck to paycheck has become the norm for us, and I have become a pro at juggling the monthly bills. I would love to sell absolutely everything in our house and live by the bare, and I mean bare, essentials. I would love to embrace this and am a little bitter and disgusted that we have gotten to this point in our lives. My needing to spend and have things has caused us problems, in our home, our marriage, and our finances and with our family life. I am hopeful that "less" will become a part of our daily life.

The Financial Impact: Your Money Woes Never Go Away

The path to happiness starts with you owning the life you have. Until you take no less than 100 percent responsibility for your life—and your choices, your debt, your failures, your disappointments, your unhappiness, and so on—you won't ever gain financial freedom. This also means you have to take responsibility for bringing everyone who is part of your life into your problem-solving equation and inspire others to make the changes necessary to achieve your shared vision.

The Solution: Open Up, Speak Up, and Take Charge

It's easy to avoid, procrastinate, put off for tomorrow, or simply ig-nore our problems. It's much harder to face them head on like a warrior and confront all the baggage that goes with them. Once you stop playing the blame game and just deal with the situation at hand by taking decisive action, you will notice a difference for the better pretty quickly. Focus less on your negative thoughts and feelings. Instead, commit to taking action today and then watch what hap-pens to those thoughts and feelings. With clarity comes focus and with focus you will move toward a greater sense of real happiness, peace, and sense of fulfillment.

What You Need to Do Today

It's easy to wallow in negativity and self-doubt, rather than to em-brace the tough change that may be necessary to turn your life around. Small steps consistently applied yield huge results. Identify an area where you can achieve a small victory, whether it's organiz-ing your sock drawer, saving the money that you spend each day on a triple latte, taking just ten extra minutes each morning for yourself to meditate, exercise, or write in a journal, or working to pay down one credit card bill. One small accomplishment in any of these areas will demonstrate that you can effect change in your life and lay the foundation for larger, more significant victories.

Excuse #5: But I Deserve the Life I Imagine Now

Like a baby who's been deprived of its bottle we all feel cheated when we can't get what we want. If there's one thing we've gotten horribly bad at, it's delayed gratification. We want everything and we want it all now. We've come to expect the best and expect we deserve to have the best when we want it—regardless of the cost. The now-famous Bing study, performed by the psychologist Walter Mischel, Ph.D. at

Stanford in the late 1960s and early 1970s showed what the effects of patience and self-control can be for human achievement. (Bing Nursery School sits on the Stanford University campus, where it partly serves as a laboratory school used by hundreds of psychology and education faculty and students. Much of the seminal research in early childhood development over the last forty years has originated there.) Dr. Mischel invented a test for children in which they were given a marshmallow but told that if they waited to eat the marshmallow until he returned to the room they could earn an extra marshmallow. Flash forward several years, when Mischel followed up with the kids in his experiment. The ones who waited, who could delay their gratification, turned out to be more successful in life—better jobs, better exam results, better coping skills, less drug addiction, and so on.

So there's something to be said for practicing personal restraint and a little self-control, even as adults. Especially as adults. The last decade gave us permission to forget about limits, and now it's time to bring those back and tame our overblown and immature sense of entitlement. None of us is entitled to a good life. It comes with hard work. We have to earn it.

The Financial Impact: You Deserve Your Debt, Too

If you think you deserve everything you want in life, and you live like that, then you deserve your debt, too. And it's probably really big, isn't it? Massive, I bet. Good luck getting that debt under control if you hold onto your entitlements. That sense of entitlement will crush any effort you make to change so you have to let it go. Getting everything you want is costing you way too much—in time, energy, happiness, and money.

The Solution: Get Real about What You Deserve

Lose the sense of entitlement. Don't look at the Joneses and waste time comparing what they have to what you don't. Focus on what you need to survive and stop whining about what you think you deserve. Chances are when you look at the two you'll notice how you already own so much more than you need to survive. And chances are you'll realize how little all that stuff actually adds to your life. Practice more self-control and reengage that inner ability to delay your gratification until you *do,* in fact, deserve it. While you can certainly dream of what you want to have in the future, don't expect to get it without effort and action. And be careful what you wish for. Living large can make for some unintended consequences. During the last boom, the size of the average new house ballooned. At the same time, the average American's waistline expanded. Today's adult is now at least twenty pounds heavier than someone of the same age pre-boom era. In the late 1970s, 15 percent of Americans were obese; now a third are.

You have to learn to justify what you think you deserve. Make sure those justifications are legitimate and play a part not just in your happiness, but also in your ability to move forward in life and be productive and successful through hard work. As Vince Lombardi once said, "The dictionary is the only place that success comes before work."

What You Need to Do Today

Make a list of things you think you deserve. Then put that list away and finish this book. When you come back to the list you will probably have a very different attitude about what you feel you deserve. What can you take off the list? Has anything changed in your thinking that allows you to recategorize a want/desire from a true need? Can you get to a point where you don't have *any* sense of entitlement?

You need to stop and think carefully about every purchase you make. Why do you deserve this? Why do you need to own this? How is owning it going to change your life? What are you replacing with this thing you so desperately want to buy? How many things like this do you already own? How are you going to pay for it?

Establish a forty-eight-hour rule for all big purchases—when you see a big ticket item that you want, wait two days before purchasing it. If you think you absolutely have to have it and it's the only one in the world, put it on hold. Then go home and write down answers to the questions above. Go online and look at your bank account and credit card bills and estimate how much that item—even if it's a huge bargain—will cost you if you don't pay cash. Do you really deserve more debt and more clutter? I don't think so either.

Excuse #6: It's Too Overwhelming

This excuse should be in all capital letters because it lies at the root of every single excuse in the book, including ones that I haven't called out yet and which belong to you (trust me, there are a lot of creative clutters!).

I know someone who is prone to migraines. When her life got crazy busy and her commitments at work became more than she could handle, a migraine was usually well underway. Once the migraine hit, she was pretty much out of commission for the couple of days it took for her to recover. She had a good sense of the warning signs, but sometimes life got in the way of her efforts to minimize the impact of the migraines until it was too late.

All of us get overwhelmed from time to time. It's a fact of modern life. Some of us experience physical manifestations of being overwhelmed in the form of headaches, stomach problems, anxiety, insomnia, full-blown panic attacks, and so on. Others may react emotionally by choosing to shut down as a way to avoid their problems. My friend with the migraines can't afford to be sick for long, or have a relapse, so she realized she had to get a handle on her health and stop the cycle of pain. Now she pays attention to the warning signs and gives herself a chance to rest. She stops running around and lets the stress go. Even though it's helped she still gets headaches on occasion. But now, when she begins to feel better, instead of jumping right back into the work she reengages slowly. And instead of letting things overwhelm her all over again, she now breaks her work down into simple, manageable steps. She keeps her physical needs a number one priority and balances out her commitments so as not to disturb her vulnerable brain.

I know that the thought of dealing with your money troubles and other "clutter" is overwhelming. How can it not be? I also know that life in general is overwhelming, regardless of your financial woes and overstuffed closets. But I can't impress upon you enough how much you will diminish the "It's Overwhelming" factor in your life once you gain control of that clutter and debt. That's what I'm trying to help you do. Life is a headache, but dealing with your clutter and financial disorder should lessen—not add to—that headache.

Time and again the people I deal with attribute much of the conflict in their relationships to their sense of being overwhelmed by the clutter in their lives. Instead of developing and deepening a relationship based on mutual respect, love, shared experiences, and happiness, I constantly see couples whose lives are torn apart by arguments about disorganization. Many of these people also struggle with anxiety or depression. All of these things are linked—where you live, what you have, and how you feel. If you feel overwhelmed, powerless, and paralyzed by the sheer volume of "the stuff" surrounding you, how can you have harmonious relationships? Where is your sense of peace if you feel defeated by what's in your own home? Instead of adding to the peace and balance of your life, your material possessions are causing stress, anxiety, unhappiness, and possibly even physical illness. They're making your emotional life harder than it needs to be. They are denying you peace of mind. Security. Happiness. Harmony. And, yes, wealth.

The Financial Impact:
Your Money Problems Remain Overwhelming and Expand

Being overwhelmed from any standpoint has the sneaky effect of paralyzing you on all fronts. Any clutter you keep in your life will have a direct hit on your financial well-being. I've watched this happen to people who are relatively financially sound. Once any area of their life becomes overwhelming, their finances become an innocent bystander. And once money problems commence, they usually continue to grow rapidly out of control, impacting everything else such as relationships, job productivity, and even personal health.

The Solution: Chunk It Down to Manageable Size

Remember, small steps yield big results. You don't have to tackle everything all in one fell swoop. Getting a handle on your life won't happen overnight. As with most major accomplishments, this will take a consistent input of energy, determination, and patience over time. Focus less on how long it may take you, and give yourself credit for just taking every step, however small, you need to move forward. Work for small changes each day and have faith that the big ones will come.

What You Need to Do Today

- Prioritizing your time and tasks is a key step in organizing your day. Write up a plan of what needs to be done, and be as specific as possible about what will get done and when. Try to build consistency into your plan of action, because research shows that the little things we do regularly, like exercising or tending to our gardens, can have a major impact on our happiness.
- Start every day with a list. Become a person who works methodically. If new tasks crop up during the day, add them to the list in order of priority.
- Commit to spending just ten minutes twice a day to decluttering your personal spaces.
- Identify your stressors—what are they? How could you reduce that stress? What specifically needs to be done? Commit to spending an hour a day over one week on two of these stressors. Schedule that time in your calendar.

- Set aside ten minutes at the start of your day to sit quietly and imagine your day as you'd like it to be. And set aside ten minutes at the end of every day to review how your day went and to make a quick mental plan for the next day. If you prepare you will be more in control of every day.

FACE FEARS AND DITCH DENIAL

Do you feel more ready to move forward now? How are you feeling so far about the things we've covered? Are you still afraid to let go of the clutter and the debt because without them you won't have any more excuses not to be living your best life? Are you still afraid that without shopping and giving yourself what you want you'll have to face *why* you need to always reward yourself with things that don't enrich you?

It comes down to this. Your home and your financial standing are a direct reflection of who you are. I don't mean that you need a showy home and a dozen high-limit credit cards to prove to the world how great you are. Your home and financial health reflect your inner life and your inner health. How content you are. How fulfilled you are. How loving and loved you are. Your home is the outward expression of what you value, what you enjoy, and what is important to you. Similarly, how you spend money and manage it mirrors how you value and respect yourself and your loved ones.

One of the overarching goals of this book is to show you how to make space for what really matters by facing those fears and ditching denial once and for all. My hope is that you'll work on your troubled relationships. You'll put an end to the health challenges that are largely preventable and the result of your choice in lifestyle. You won't ignore your children's emotional—and physical—needs. You'll fess up to your issues with work or your job potential. You'll dream big. And you'll learn to live big within your means—both financial and physical. I know that these are all massively large things to accomplish, and none of them will happen overnight or by the end of this book. But if you keep reminding yourself to be patient as you reach your vision through small, methodical steps using all the strategies in this book (plus any others you discover on your own!), then you'll feel empowered. You'll see all of this as doable no matter how monumental your vision may seem right now.

PERSONAL ACTION PLAN FOR YOUR LIFE

Get clarity: Organizing your life isn't just about simplifying and "cleaning up" its various components. It's about having a vision, setting new priorities, being mindful of your time, and using those notions to change the habits and behaviors that continue to hold you back and strangle your dreams.

Get real: Stop being a victim. The clutter in your life is yours and yours alone, even if you share your life (and some of that clutter) with others. Don't cling to your problems in the form of anger and frustration instead of letting go and changing. By the same token, don't let your clutter overwhelm or paralyze you to the point of inaction. Take responsibility—for your vision and your clutter.

Get going: Make a commitment today to figure out what's really bothering you in your life and make it a goal to change that. Start with the question: Where is the tension in my life? See where that takes you. Then work your way backward to create small, doable goals to remove that tension. Look at how you're spending your time and rethink your priorities. And if you need just one thing to do today . . .

A task for today: Sit down with a journal and a calendar. Write down the single biggest source of tension in your life in the journal, then turn to the calendar and pick one day—just one day—in the future where you will have done *something* to address that tension. Maybe it's a conversation with your partner. Maybe it's scheduling a meeting with a financial planner. And maybe it's just giving yourself permission to let go of your old dreams of living large and accepting that living on less can amount to living a much richer, fuller, and deeply satisfying life. Make a conscious choice to live on less. Focus on having a life of quality, not quantity.

The Financial Audit: Your Money

USING MONEY OF YOUR OWN and using money that belongs to someone else are two very different things—even though you can buy exactly the same items no matter the source of the cash. It's easy to forget that the credit cards you own or the credit line you have is not your money. Looked at a little differently, there is a huge difference between how much you have and how much you have *access* to. For example, you may have a home filled with things but little in the way of funds to help pay for more education. Or you could be driving an expensive car with all the extras and have the latest technology at your fingertips but your dream to travel the world and access new cultures has been on hold forever because you can't ever seem to afford the trip.

Far too often we believe the point of having money is to help us aquire material possessions and that those material possessions will afford us happiness. Thinking this way disregards money's true source of power: to give us access to what can propel us forward in life. And it's the journey of moving forward that makes us happy— not the money itself. Money affords us opportunities to learn more about the world and ourselves, to seek more knowledge and skills, to have the freedom to go where we want to go, and to live independently. Many of us have lost this distinction between money's relation to acquisition and money's relation to *access*. After all, wouldn't you rather have access to more information, more freedom, and more independence than just more things? Wouldn't you prefer to have access to the best health insurance and the best care for your family?

Considering the fact that owning more things can pin you down to more obligations, more debt, and cost you time and energy by diverting your attention away from other more important—and definitely more life-enhancing—activities, you can begin to see how owning less stuff and having more access is the real secret power of money. In the last several years, consumerism took control and disempowered us. Now we must regain that control and learn how to use money to its fullest advantage. When you have money in the bank and your bills are consistently paid in full, your options open up. Rather than servicing debt, you can have the security and means to put money toward fulfilling your dreams, such as taking classes, traveling abroad, or helping your kids enrich their own lives with things like extra coaching or music lessons. Money at your fingertips that doesn't have to go toward debt is empowering.

Getting to that place, however, where you can unleash the real power of money begins with a financial audit. Why? Because you need to come face to face with how much money you have and how much money you owe in order to know what you're dealing with. This audit will help you take the pulse of your financial health. If you've done a version of this exercise in the past, I still want you to do it again here. Unlike other financial audits you may have done before, you're not going to consider just the numbers and figures. Here you'll confront the underlying feelings, emotions, and frustrations that all those numbers give you. Remember, financial clutter can be just as taxing to your well-being—if not more so—than physical clutter. You may be frightened that you're about to open a can of worms or Pandora's box. Don't panic. We'll move through this step by step together.

FIRST THINGS FIRST

You know what you need to do first: call up the vision you've created for the life you want. Really focus on it and be very clear about it. Now add to it by defining your vision for the financial life you want. Think about specific goals you have in mind to fulfill that financial vision. I'll give you a list of ideas for inspiration to get you going, and then you can use the chart that follows to detail your own ideas. Think about the vision you have for yourself within a year from now, five years from now, and ten years from now. Pay attention to how closely your overall life vision relates to your financial vision. Be realistic. Don't tell yourself that you can pay off all your debts and buy your dream home in a year if you're looking at 100K in debt and have no savings. Remember, no choice is made in a vacuum; make sure any steps you take are financially responsible and appropriate to your situation. Here are some examples of goals my clients have made in the past:

- Downsize to a smaller home with a more manageable mortgage I can pay off in fifteen years or less. (1 year)
- Avoid foreclosure and get my mortgage back on track. (1 year)
- Zero credit card debt. (5 years)
- Zero student loans. (5 years)
- Max out my retirement accounts every year.
- Have money saved for an annual vacation to an exotic destination. (5 years)
- Buy a second home in the mountains I can use for ski season and rent out. (10 years)
- Pay for my children's education through college. (10 years)
- Retire by the age of sixty. (10+ years)
- Not have to think and worry so much about money. (Today!)
- Be happy with what I already own.

WHAT DOES *YOUR* FINANCIAL
PICTURE LOOK LIKE IN . . .

List out specific—realistic—goals you have under each time frame.
Shoot for at least five goals for each period of time.

1 Year

_____

_____

_____

_____

5 Years

_____

_____

_____

_____

10 Years

_____

_____

_____

_____

GET EVERYONE ON BOARD TODAY (IF YOU HAVEN'T ALREADY!)

You knew that you wouldn't get away with doing these exercises alone and not have to drag your family members into the loop at some point. Most of us don't find money the most romantic and family-friendly topic of conversation, but the problems that come with financial clutter are real and worth clearing away as a team. They are also rarely caused by a single member of the family.

It's up to you how much you want to share the details of your financial situation with your children. I say, the more you do, the merrier you can all be in the end. Just be sure that you give your kids age-appropriate information tailored to their needs and capacity. Also, ensure that you and your partner work through any highly sensitive and emotional issues regarding your money issues first before you bring the kids into the picture.

Have you had that initial conversation yet with your partner? If your attitudes toward spending are wildly diverse from your partner's, the best way to resolve them is on paper. Instead of criticizing money choices, decide on your financial goals together. You need to have a shared vision for your finances in the same way you need to have a shared vision of the home you want and the life you imagine for yourselves. In both cases the clear vision comes before you decide how best to deal with the clutter—financial or otherwise. Calculate what you need to save to reach your vision. Once you establish your goals, you will know how much money you can spend on luxuries. Only at that point should you start to discuss what level of spending is reasonable and how to manage it.

WHAT DOES YOUR *FAMILY'S*
FINANCIAL PICTURE LOOK LIKE IN . . .

List out specific—realistic—goals you have under each time frame.
Shoot for at least five goals for each period of time.

1 Year

_____

_____

_____

_____

5 Years

_____

_____

_____

_____

10 Years

_____

_____

_____

_____

Be sure to link specific goals to certain family members where appropriate. For example, if your son will be going off to college within five years, then you may want to add "help pay for Johnny's college tuition" under the column "5 years." Similarly, if you know the financial demands of raising your daughter will change significantly once she reaches school age in a year, then you may want to list that out: "Pay for Lucy's ballet and piano lessons without incurring debt."

Here's something else to think about: What have you had to reluctantly give up due to your money woes? What hardship has your family endured in exchange for immediate gratification and the excessive debt it creates? Which of the following situations have you experienced? Review each statement below and check the ones that apply to you now or have applied to your financial circumstances in the recent past:

❑ Can't take a family trip or vacation because you just don't have the money.

❑ Can't take advantage of a business opportunity because you lack the funds.

❑ Live in constant fear because you can't see the light at the end of this money tunnel.

❑ Can't give your children what they really need to live better and have a safer future.

❑ Can't change or leave your job because of debts.

❑ Have gone without proper insurance on your car or have had to forgo buying medical insurance for you or your family.

❑ Have had sleepless nights, bouts of anxiety and depression that you hide from your family and friends.

❑ Can't give gifts during the holidays or other celebrations.

❑ Fear going out with friends because any collective bill will be split evenly.

❑ Made excuses when someone wants to visit you because you can't handle paying to entertain them.

No one should have to live in such fear and avoid the simple pleasures of spending time with friends and providing for the family just because of money problems. So now comes the hard part toward rectifying all this.

LET'S GO DIGGING

Clear a space for this exercise and gather your most recent financial statements. If you have twenty years' worth of tax returns and ten years' worth of receipts stored in boxes somewhere, forget those for now. Just focus on the documents that will help you to paint a current financial picture. These include: bank account statements, credit card bills, loans, mortgages, and all your monthly bills. For some of you this will be harder than for others. If the statements are buried in piles of paper, don't worry about anything else in that pile right now, just dig out what you need and deal with the rest later. (Note: this is not the time to organize your files. You can do that later.) If your accounts are online, print out your most recent monthly statement and also write the balance in your account right now on a piece of paper. This will help you see patterns in your spending (outside of bills) and it can show you how much money you really have right now. If you have a pile of unopened bills (because you know there are notices about long-overdue invoices in there) then open those up and get them on the table.

Divide all of your statements into two piles and tally them up:

COLUMN A. WHAT YOU HAVE

Savings accounts (including certificates of deposit)   _____

Checking accounts   _____

401(k), IRA, or other retirement account   _____

Investment and brokerage (stocks, bonds, options,
money market funds, mutual funds)   _____

Other investments or accounts (annuities, cash value
of life insurance)   _____

Other (cash, car, real estate, business interest, antiques,
art, tax refunds, valuable sporting and hobby equipment,
electronic equipment, jewelry, collectibles, and any other
major assets, money owed to you by others)   _____

TOTAL: _____

COLUMN B. WHAT YOU OWE

Outstanding credit card bills   _____

Loans (mortgage, car, student, business, promissory
note/personal loans, home equity line)   _____

Other unpaid bills (utilities, cable, medical, vet, telephone,
cell phone, retail store cards, gas cards, back taxes)   _____

Any other debts   _____

TOTAL: _____

> **Extra Credit:** If you want extra credit for doing this audit, then I recommend finding out your credit score as well. This can easily be done with the click of a mouse at AnnualCredit Report.com. This is the official site where you can obtain your credit report once every twelve months for free from each of the nationwide consumer credit reporting companies: Equifax, Experian, and TransUnion.

Now, if you really want to know what your net worth is, you could subtract the total in column B from the total in column A, but I won't make you do that. Not only is your net worth not a very helpful planning a financial strategy, but your mortgage could be throwing everything off depending on exactly how much you owe. If you sold your house today, what you owe would radically change. Instead, what I want you to do is evaluate your emotions at this point.

Start with column A. Study it carefully and then ask yourself: How does this make me feel? Secure? Insecure? Scared? Empty? In good shape? Strong? Weak?

> Write down a word or two here that reflects your feelings when reading column A: _____
>
> _____
>
> Do the same for column B: _____
>
> _____

However you feel, do not think in terms of good and bad, and don't view one side as good and the other evil, no matter what your gut instinct is telling you. You may have a respectable reason to have a huge discrepancy between the two columns, but you may not. A medical emergency may have set you back last year, and there are good sources of debt. Student loans, investment in a sound business through a loan, and mortgages are all considered forms of healthy debt when used properly.

Column C: What You Own That You Don't Use or Can't Sell

Pretend that there's another column in the chart where you list your big ticket purchases for the last year—electronics, designer brand clothing, shoes, furniture, sporting equipment, motor vehicles. You get the idea. List all those expensive items that you bought but cannot sell for what you paid. This column may also entail items that you've bought but don't use. Examples include furniture stored in the garage or basement, clothes in your closet with the tags still attached, items in your kitchen drawers that you've never used, toys in your children's rooms that are never played with, gifts that you've purchased for other people but never given away, and linens or other household items bought on sale that have never been used and which remain in their original wrappings.

Take one room at a time and add up the cost of these unused or seldom-used items. These aren't necessarily "assets" because you cannot sell them for nearly as much as what you paid for them (we're talking pennies on the dollar if you manage to sell them online or at a consignment store). Seeing just how much you have that is of little value (even to you because you don't use them!) may be an eye-opening experience.

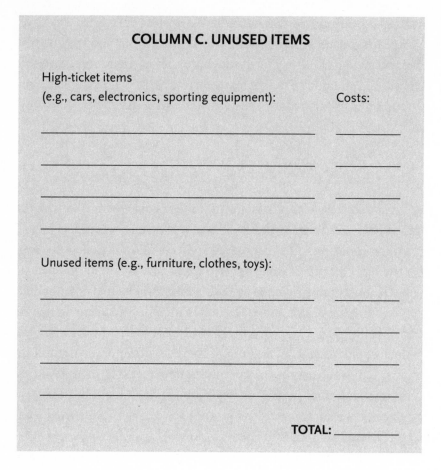

COLUMN C. UNUSED ITEMS

High-ticket items
(e.g., cars, electronics, sporting equipment):   Costs:

_____   _____

_____   _____

_____   _____

_____   _____

Unused items (e.g., furniture, clothes, toys):

_____   _____

_____   _____

_____   _____

_____   _____

TOTAL: _____

Think of all that money you'd have in your pocket now if you'd never purchased these items to begin with. These things have stolen your living space and robbed your bank account. From now on, when you have the urge to spend money on other, similar items to fill your home, think about this column C and remind yourself: *I don't really need this! It will only add to my clutter and sabotage the financial vision I have for myself.*

Something else to keep in mind when looking at all this stuff: recall how entitled you felt to purchase these items at one time. Do you feel entitled to them now? Did this sense of entitlement lead to happiness? Do your purchases hold the same "value" to you now as they appeared to have then? How has your connection to these items—and your sense of need versus want—changed over time? My guess is you no longer feel a strong sense of connection to them, nor a need to even have them in your life now. This is a tough but valuable lesson—even if it does come at a steep price!

TRACK YOUR EXPENSES

If you look at your bills and are still not sure where your money is going, you should itemize a month's worth of expenses. What you discover about yourself when you do this will help you understand a lot about how you spend your money and will help you figure out how to make changes. You can track just your credit card purchases or do a more rigorous financial audit of all your spending using the chart below. Do your best to be extra meticulous for just one month. It's a lesson that has big rewards. Keep all your receipts and create receipts for items when you don't get one, which happens a lot when we use cash. Carry a small spiral notepad in your purse or back pocket to jot down every cent you spend, no matter how insignificant it may seem. There are also several applications that you can download online or through a smart phone and to help you to track your expenses.

Alternatively, you can create a spreadsheet in a program like Excel, using the categories listed below (or copy this chart as many times as you need). Drop your data into it for at least one month. You'll then be able to draw basic conclusions about where your money goes. And then you can more confidently take the proper action. Note that several of the expenses below only get paid on a weekly, monthly, or even annual basis.

LIFE TRACKING

Food	Mon	Tue	Wed	Thur	Fri	Sat	Sun	Total
groceries								
breakfast								
lunch								
dinner								
snacks								
guest								
other								
Totals								

Shelter	Weekly or Monthly Totals
housing (rent/mortgage)	
phone	
gas and electric	
water/garbage	
cable/internet	

Shelter (cont.)	Weekly or Monthly Totals
household items	
insurance	
housekeeper	
property taxes	
homeowner dues	
repair/maintenance	
other	
Totals	

Self-Care	Weekly or Monthly Totals
clothing	
shoes	
accessories	
hair care	
toiletries	
manicure/pedicure	

Self-Care (cont.)	Weekly or Monthly Totals
medical/health	
dry cleaning/laundry	
life/disability insurance	
gym	
other	
Totals	

Dependent Care	Weekly or Monthly Totals
clothes	
child care	
child tuition	
pets	
other	
Totals	

Transportation	Weekly or Monthly Totals
car payment	

Transportation (cont.)	Weekly or Monthly Totals
gas	
maintenance	
parking/tolls	
bus or other	
other	
Totals	

Entertainment	Weekly or Monthly Totals
movies	
concerts/theater	
dating	
subscriptions	
other	
Totals	

Investments	Weekly or Monthly Totals
savings	

Investments (cont.)	Weekly or Monthly Totals
vacation	
retirement	
other	
Totals	

Other Monthly Allocations	Weekly or Monthly Totals
taxes	
car registration	
other	
Totals	

Miscellaneous	Weekly or Monthly Totals
Totals	

Debt Repayment	Weekly or Monthly Totals
Totals	

One-Time Expenses	Weekly or Monthly Totals
Totals	

GRAND TOTALS

If you run your own business, you should do this same exercise for your business separately. Be sure to include office supplies, shipping and postage, rented or leased equipment, and any other expenses related to your business that are not listed above.

• • •

Looking at your tracking record now in conjunction with the inventory you took of what you owe and your financial resources, ask yourself the following questions:

EVALUATING YOUR TRACKING

- How well am I using money? _____
- Am I spending more than I'm making? _____
- Is this a record of someone who overspends or someone who uses money—and debt—wisely? _____
  _____
- Do I have healthy debt (e.g., mortgage, school loans) or mostly unhealthy debt (e.g., credit card balances, unpaid bills, collections, debts used to support a lifestyle)? _____
- Am I financially fit or totally out of shape? _____
- Do I live for the moment and assume the future will take care of itself, or does it look like I plan for the future and have control of it? _____
- Do I have a lot of unnecessary expenses under one-time expenses, entertainment, and self-care? _____
- Does this record make me confident or frightened? Happy or sad? _____
- My weakest spot is: _____
- One thing I can change this week to get back on track (i.e., an expense to be mindful of) is: _____

Dear Peter:
We have financial clutter! We have bills scattered around the house and debt all over the place. We are not organized paying our bills and therefore have carelessly spent hundreds on

late fees and overdrafts. It's embarrassing and frustrating. My husband and I get stressed about it. Though we don't usually fight about money, we do experience depression and tension because of our lack of funds. Neither of us has huge spending habits, mainly because we can't, our car note (only one, the other is paid off) is reasonable, our house note is a little high, but not outrageous. We make close to $100,000 per year and we can't seem to make it. What is wrong with us? We've had to borrow money from my mother a few times and had to forgo social outings with our friends because we can't afford to participate. Our children are still small, so they don't really know what is happening and for that I am *very* grateful. This is not a stress I want them to have—*ever*! We want to get this handled before long because it is affecting our quality of life.

Right about now you may be feeling a rush of unwelcome emotions. Be patient and let those emotions come. They are there for a reason and you have to give yourself time to feel them and examine them to understand what they mean. I'm not asking you to do this audit just to make you feel bad about your spending habits or the fact that you're knee-deep in debt. Remember that the goal here is to get the information you need to execute the strategies for living out your vision. Think of these audits as tools you're collecting in your toolbox that you'll use to shape and build your vision. Despite the emotional upheaval they may cause, these audits are invaluable to you and your future.

This particular financial audit should help you focus on where your pursuit of "more" is taking over your life and robbing you of true happiness. We don't buy just for necessity. We also buy because a strong emotional undercurrent fuels our spending habits (and remember that habits are habitual, something that you repeat over and over again). When you itemize your spending it becomes very clear exactly where your money is going. Is it on dinners out? Clothes? Collectibles? Unnecessary home renovations and decorations? Vacations? Chasing bargains? Presents for your spouse and kids? How do your emotions tie into your purchasing habits? For example, do you get up every Saturday and rush to the mall to avoid spending time with your spouse? Do you spend your evenings online, buying things you don't need so you can feel better about yourself? Do you look around your house and think it's not the vision of perfection the magazines and shows tell you it should be so you keep buying new things hoping to achieve that perfection? Shopping is a means to an end. If it's an end in itself then there's a problem.

I've already mentioned that you're not alone in this mess. America has a problem with debt and overaccumulation. We live in one of the most prosperous nations on the planet and we've come to measure our success by material accumulation. We have come to believe that our purchases will buy us happiness, tranquility, peace, an easier life, less stress, more efficiency, greater success, optimal health, and so on.

Sometimes what we choose to buy does, in fact, give us those things. But as you can probably tell by looking at your financial picture now, the vast majority of your purchases has had the opposite effect of what you had hoped for. When you reviewed your credit card statements, you likely came across purchases you're still paying for but get nothing out of anymore. There's nothing intrinsically wrong with spending money on educational or entertaining things that may not last forever, but where do you draw the line? What do you have to show at the end of the year for all the money you have spent? There's no getting around the truth that we tend to spend money on very little that has lasting value and that can truly add to the quality of our life over the long term. As I pointed out earlier, we frequently acquire things we think we need for survival, but there are very few things we actually need in order to survive.

Which brings me to the undeniable outcome of all that excess spending: serious stress, emotional trauma, and family drama over money issues. Suddenly, you're at odds with your partner over money, your kids over money, and even yourself. Money, especially when it's not there for us when we need it, becomes such a major source of conflict. Surely you know this without me having to prove it to you. Which is why this process is so emotional and hard on your heart. But once you face your financials, you've already taken that first step in lightening your load—both literally and emotionally. The work you'll do in this next chapter will help you take this leap forward.

6

Face the Financials

HAVING A HOME FILLED WITH STUFF doesn't conceal money problems. Much to the contrary, clutter exposes financial mayhem like nothing else. I have never visited a cluttered home that wasn't standing on shaky financial ground as well. You can't live in a home that's physically out of balance unless your spending habits are out of balance, too.

Recall what I said earlier about living in a culture that sends very clear messages about what we have, what we don't have, and what we *should* have. In our society, success is demonstrated by acquiring more and having better. We embrace outward signs of success through acquisition and possession rather than an inner feeling of happiness and well-being. This wayward thinking has led us down the "more is better" path of self-absorption and, for some, self-destruction. Once on this path it's not so difficult to move farther from our authentic selves and deeper into the scary unknowns of endless debt.

Debt is sneaky. It's a silent killer like the plaque that clogs your arteries. It descends on you when you least expect it (usually in your promising youth when the world is your proverbial oyster) and slowly builds up over time until it's massive and seemingly too monstrous to overcome. It's not just an obstacle that impedes your life, but it also has the power to destroy it. Debt erodes your creditworthiness, your sense of security, your independence, your happiness, and, as I've been telling you since the beginning of this book, your relationships and sense of self.

If you have credit card debt and no idea how to get rid of it, you're not alone. You're also not alone if what's happened in the last couple of years has *un*motivated you to do anything about it. As we hear more war stories on Wall Street about the depths of our recession and combined debt as a nation, a part of us can grow numb. We no longer see it as an individual problem, but rather a collective problem—a Main Street (and mainstream) problem—that should be solved as such. After all, if everyone else is in debt then how can it be so bad? Why should I worry so much about my debt if no one else is? Aren't we all in the same boat? Debt is the new normal, right? If the government says everything will be okay no matter what, even though it could be a long recovery, is that true? Maybe debt isn't so bad after all!

Wrong. I'm here to tell you straight up that this kind of thinking is dangerous. Yes, you and your fellow Americans are equally trapped in the same financial quicksand, but looking to others—the government, your governor, your neighbor, or avoiding looking at your debt at all—will sink you faster than you can cry "where's the next sale?" But sidestepping the issue, saying it's someone else's problem, and waiting for everything to be solved by someone else at some imaginary future date is a huge mistake. Take responsibility. It's your only way out.

If the financial audit you just took left a mess of paperwork (worse than what you started with), and you're reading this with one eye closed because the mere thought of facing your financials is too terrifying, relax. Just as we did before with the personal clutter, we're going to take it slow and we're going to attempt to order your thoughts first. Yes, this involves revisiting your vision again. This will give you a source of inspiration that will help you set a strong foundation for coming to grips with and managing your finances.

TAKE A LOOK AT THAT FINANCIAL VISION AGAIN

Look back for a moment at the financial vision you started to outline for yourself on page 120. What does your financial picture look like in one year, five years, and ten years? When do you want to retire or do something else? What realistic goals did you set up for yourself? How will others in your life have to contribute to these goals and this overall vision? Are they playing the part now or will you have to enlist more help and support from them? Are you being honest with yourself about what you can and cannot do, and what's realistic in terms of your resources and ideal time frame? How do your current behaviors and attitudes affect this vision for good or bad? Will *you* have to change in order to make this all happen?

Spend a little more time now really thinking about that financial vision you briefly sketched out before. Bring your current financial situation into the picture, too. Remember, when you considered your financial vision earlier in the book, you hadn't yet taken your financial audit. Now that you have, this vision might need some tweaking. Really think about how much money you make, what you spend it on, and what your financial goals are. Keep those thoughts in mind as you complete the following exercise.

QUIZ: ME AND MY FINANCIALS

My current financial situation is:
- ❑ better than I expected
- ❑ worse than I expected

Words that describe the financial situation I *want* to have:

_____

Words that describe the financial situation I *currently* have:

_____

What I need to feel safe: _____

_____

Major expenses that I may face in the near future: _____

_____

Major expenses that I may face in the long term: _____

_____

What I want to do when I retire from my current job: _____

_____

What I need to survive when I retire from my current job:

_____

Five things that currently get in the way of the financial life that I imagine for myself:

1. _____

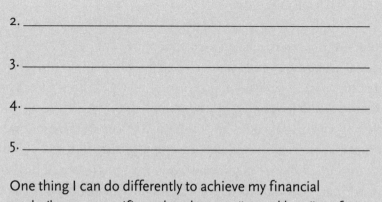

2. _____

3. _____

4. _____

5. _____

One thing I can do differently to achieve my financial
goals (be very specific; rather than say "spend less," try for
something like "stop shopping on Saturday with the kids and
take them to the park instead"): _____

_____

Are you living your dream, or do you fantasize about a future
lifestyle that's totally different from the one you're currently living?
Do you wish you could afford more vacations? Where would you like
to live? Are you hoping to move to somewhere warm and sunny or
to settle into a quiet suburb? Would you like to leave your job for one
that earns less money but is more fulfilling? Can you afford to do so?
Do you anticipate retiring one day? How will you live? Will you take
cruises? See movies and plays frequently? Will you finally become a
wine expert? What kind of car will you drive? Will you pursue long-
delayed hobbies? Well, guess what—you can't pay for your fantasies
with play money. You must make your future happen through calcu-
lated, conscious steps today.

LIFE IS FULL OF OPTIONS

From now on, see if you can view money as your golden key in life, the tool that gains you access to whatever you want within reasonable limits. The exercise you just completed would have a totally different outcome if you had all the money in the world, wouldn't it? Some of your fears would be gone and you wouldn't have to worry so much about major expenses and "just getting by." But we know that having all the money in the world isn't possible and having it doesn't instantly make you happier. Having money doesn't change who you are or how you behave, and suddenly becoming a millionaire wouldn't change the core reasons you have issues with money now. Money is a means to an end—not an end in itself. And unless you understand it and your relationship to it, you will never use it well, no matter how little or how much you have.

What I want for you is to have plenty with which you not just survive but *thrive*. This is possible when you contemplate your needs, wants, hopes, and dreams and translate those desires into dollars and cents. It's possible when you regard your limits, make preparations for worst-case scenarios (e.g., accidents, illness, job loss, family troubles, and so on), and learn to appreciate money as your full access pass. Remember, money saved isn't just security, it's options. Regardless of your salary, your future income potential, and your earning power, you can have a better life.

FINANCIAL ILLITERACY AND THE FEAR FACTOR

If you need to blame someone for your current financial state, I'll let you vent about the fact no one ever sat you down when you first knew what money was to tell you about how it all works. Unfortunately, we don't teach our children financial literacy in school so most of us grow up learning about money through trial and error. Imagine taking a final exam as a sixth grader where one of the questions is: If

I owe $100 to company X, and the company is charging 30 percent interest on that balance each month, how much will I owe in two years if I don't make any payments until then? I think we'd be having a different conversation today if financial literacy were as standard in school as learning to read.

When we lack certain knowledge we think we should have, what happens? We get scared. If you don't know how to swim, being near deep water is frightening. If you don't know how to fly an airplane, being at the controls in a cockpit and told to take off would be terrifying. And this is how it is with money. If you don't know how to manage money well, the whole topic is scary, from the more mundane actions of paying bills and keeping a checkbook balanced to the more sophisticated dealings such as investing in the stock market and managing a portfolio.

Most of us are scared of money. The easiest thing to do is to put your paycheck in your bank account, spend what you want, and hope for the best. But the wisest thing to do is to be aware of in- and outflow, to clear up bad debt, and to invest your savings so that your money grows over time. There's really nothing to be scared of, but fear is the biggest obstacle to clearing financial clutter. It's time to get over that fear.

Dear Peter:
For my family, the recession, or whatever you want to call it, was actually a blessing. When my husband's paychecks started shrinking, at first I was panicky, then I sat down and looked at where our money was going. I realized that I needed to cut back in any area possible. I started with "shopping," and I'm not talking about groceries. I just decided to stay out of stores unless I had a specific NEED on my list, and got out as quickly as possible.

I then went back to some of my prior habits that had fallen

by the wayside. Before each purchase I would ask myself these questions:

- Do we need this?
- Do we need it right now? (or will it be on sale later?)
- Where will it go? Does it have a designated place in our home?

For clothing purchases, I also have some rules:

- For every article coming into our home, another must go out.
- Don't buy more hangers; throw out things not being worn.

I also decided that there was no room in our budget for home decor. I did not say improvements, such as replacing something worn out or broken, but upgrades and things that would just look nice. We go out once each week, preferably for lunch, and the cost must be close to what a meal at home would be. Coupons are great!

When I have a hard time parting with something (usually because of its cost), I put it in a box in the middle of the living room so I will see it many times each day. I get so sick of seeing it, I am then glad to donate it to charity!

The good news is though we will only take in approximately two-thirds of last year's income, we are OK and debt free! I honestly think revisiting the budget was necessary and a very good thing. I guess sometimes it takes a crisis to give us a wake-up call.

ATTITUDE ADJUSTMENT

Most of us need an attitude adjustment on two big levels. One, we need to shift our emotional relationship with money from one of fear to one of empowerment; and two, we need to change our sense of entitlement. This isn't that hard to do. It simply requires a little education combined with some vigilant self-examination and action. Think of it this way: you can't lose weight without expending more calories than you consume, and you can't save money without spending less than you make. As with the old rule of calories in, calories out, if you earn $100 and spend $80—no problem. If you earn $100 and spend $120—there's a problem. It's that simple!

The following quiz will help you to take the temperature of your attitude around money. This will help you to see where you may need to make an attitude adjustment and work toward changing how you behave and think about money.

QUIZ: YOUR RELATIONSHIP WITH MONEY

If you had to rank your comfort level with money, on a scale of 1 to 10 (1 being low, and 10 being high), what would it be?

_____

Think of a word or two to describe your relationship with money: _____

_____

Do you think of yourself as a mathematical invalid and leave the bill paying to someone else? _____

_____

Are you intimidated by investing? _____

_____

Do you feel entitled to certain material goods, regardless of how much they cost? _____

_____

Do you hide financial records from yourself or your partner?

_____

Do you leave mail unopened and bills unpaid for longer than you know you should? _____

_____

Do you spend with no idea of how much you have or what you owe? _____

_____

Do you have something as basic as a budget in place? _____

_____

Do you spend money impulsively driven by your moods rather than your needs? _____

_____

Do guilt and regret accompany some of your spending sprees? _____

_____

When you find yourself buying like there's no tomorrow, do you ever stop to ask yourself *why?* _____

_____

What's really driving the spending? Describe your reasons for spending: _____

_____

What emotions are moving through you when you make that purchase? Choose a few words that describe what you feel when you spend money *before* the purchase: _____

_____;

and *after* the purchase: _____

_____.

Now look back at your responses. Would you say you have a healthy or unhealthy relationship with money and its uses? How do you want to change that relationship for the better?

No matter how little or how much money you earn, managing your money is simple. I'm not saying you'll never end up in the red because yes, things do happen in life. But there is always a way out. There is always a way to recover and get back out of the hole. And it all starts with cleaning up the mess you've made. If you aren't happy with your financial situation, you'll have to remove emotion from the equation when it comes to your spending decisions. You'll also have to overcome your fear of money by learning how to manage it well. Really, that's what it takes!

Get Real about Today's Needs and Wants

As I mentioned earlier, the line between wants and needs has been lost in recent times thanks to our bloated sense of entitlement. We've lost sight of what we really need to live comfortably but not excessively. We've also forgotten what "affordability" means because credit cards have nixed that word from our vocabulary. While millions in other parts of the world live on cents a day, we have the luxury—yes, the *luxury*—of an unparalleled standard of living. We live on tens, sometimes hundreds, of dollars a day. We take for granted the fact we can order food to be delivered to our door, power up computers to download music, play video games and watch movies in the comfort of our home, and drive a car to the store for food, clothing, and medicine whenever we need to. We can't imagine an existence without hot water, electricity, or functioning toilets.

The conveniences of modern life in the developed world are pretty amazing. They make life easier, but they also make it much harder to differentiate what's really necessary from what's not. Could you get by on just pennies a day? Probably not unless you were forced to. Could you go without a computer, television, car, or phone? Again, probably not unless you were forced to. I'm not asking you to embrace the ascetic life of a hermit or to forgo modern conveniences that we've all grown accustomed to, but I will ask you to become more aware of this fine line between needs and wants. And to seriously consider what's necessary and what's not. The goal for you is to appreciate what you already have, have what you need to survive, and prepare for your future by bringing your needs and wants into line with your income.

How much of your income do you truly need to survive? How much do you currently spend on food, clothing, and shelter? How much of your debt is not part of an asset or investment, such as a mortgage or student loan that funds your future? Is the majority of your debt related to frivolous purchases loading down your credit cards? What are those purchases? Are you using them every day?

Have they enhanced your life to the point that they were worth over-spending for? If you don't make monthly payments in full, you're effectively paying more every month for every item you've purchased. What seemed so necessary and such a bargain the day you bought it isn't such a deal when you're paying 25 percent interest on your credit card balance three months later.

Entitlements: Enter at Your Own Risk

None of us is entitled to things we can't afford on our own. In fact, none of us is entitled to anything if we cannot manage our money. By "managing money," I'm referring to keeping track of your income's coming and goings—spending responsibly and saving for a rainy day and many sunny days in retirement. If you've got bad credit card debt then it's time to look at what got you that debt. How many luxury items do you own? How many TVs fill your home? How many giant flat screen TVs that require expensive monthly cable service? Do you have the premium cell phone plan? How often do you eat in restaurants or order takeout? Do you drive an expensive leased car? Is your closet full of designer clothes and shoes? Is your dresser covered with jewelry, makeup, and expensive creams? How often do you take a weekend getaway or an expensive vacation? Has the pressure of owning all this stuff made you happier? I bet not. None of these things is a necessity and unless you can pay for all of these things with cold hard cash—and have plenty left over to fill your savings accounts, you shouldn't have them. And if you're serious about turning things around, these luxuries are the first things that have to go—no discussion!

Dear Peter:
I had a rude awakening when I ended up in the hospital with terrible pneumonia. That is when I realized life had to change.

We had an enormous amount of credit card debt and our family business slowed down dramatically. We were lucky enough to find a woman who helped me figure out the finances. One of the biggest no-nos I was making was going to the market almost every two days and eating out. We now eat the majority of our meals at home and it is the BEST! So much communication happens! We have learned to live within our means and slow down. We don't go out as much—we love our parks and finding new walking trails. Life is so much more simple, peaceful, and less chaotic. I hosted a family holiday and for the first time everyone did potluck and it was one of our best holidays ever. Because our business has been slow we have been clearing out our house of excess and living off of it! We just had a garage sale this past Saturday and my kids shocked me, they *picked* out the items they wanted to sell (they each made $40!!) and we had the best time.

Sure it's hard sometimes—needs and wants—I just received a gift card and was able to get the first bottle of perfume in a couple of years. Sure we need/want certain things, but we are the happiest I have ever been in my relationship and I don't feel like we have to keep up with the Joneses— I used to run away to the mall or go out to eat to escape the clutter in my house. I used to have a cleaning lady, but I am learning to love to clean. I think I used clutter to fill a void in my life. Life is great. Money and things aren't everything.

CONFRONT YOUR EXCUSES

Excuses that revolve around money are commonplace. I hear these from every walk of life. Which ones below have you used? Let's take inventory of how many you can relate to. Put a check mark next to every excuse below that you can identify with:

- ❑ But I'm a great shopper!

- ❑ But I work hard—I deserve this.

- ❑ But no one in my family is good with money—we've always been like that.

- ❑ But I'm feeling guilty/sad/upset/angry (or even happy/celebratory/excited)—buying something helps me feel better.

- ❑ _____

  (Fill in the blank with your excuse.)

Excuse #1: But I'm a great shopper!

This statement is only true if you're only buying the things you absolutely need and are not cluttering up your house or sinking your bank account. Shopping has an allure to it, no doubt. In fact, if you find the bargains you probably *are* a great shopper. But bargains and sales should not be the reason to plunk down money. Everything is always for sale and on sale, did you ever think of that? There's no such thing as a bargain if it cost you more than you can afford. Although shopping can provide lots of short-term pleasure and give you a temporary high, it can become an addiction that disregards financial means and clouds your ability to distinguish between what's necessary and what's not. This behavior rarely nourishes long-term happiness. Much to the contrary, it sets you up for long-term misery and frustration.

The Financial Impact: Broke and Broken

"Hey, Peter, you know, those bargains really add up—a few dollars here or there and pretty soon you've saved some real money." To that I ask, have you *saved* money? No, you've spent it. You've gone broke saving money! And you've neglected doing important things in your life in your pursuit of the next great sale. What this really means is you've led yourself down a path of self-destruction rather than self-fulfillment.

It doesn't matter what you paid compared to what it originally cost because your "savings" isn't real. When the item was $100 you didn't buy it because you didn't need it. Now that it's $50 you still don't need it. And no matter how great the discount, you are still shelling out your cash for it. If you go shopping the sales, pretty soon you'll find that you've "saved" yourself hundreds of dollars of debt. For things you don't need. And no matter how much you saved, if you put it on a credit card you'll wind up giving all the savings back in interest and the bargain is no longer a bargain.

The Solution: Step Away from the Instigators of Shopping

Recovering alcoholics don't sit in bars and keep six-packs in their refrigerators. Dieters don't bake chocolate cakes or walk into a fast food joint. The easiest way to get out of the habit of constantly shopping is simply to remove yourself from an environment that encourages shopping or makes it too accessible. What would you rather do: say no to something attractive staring you in the face or not have to say no because you're not subjecting yourself to the temptation?

What You Need to Do Today

Stop reading the Sunday ads in the newspaper. Drive a different way home so that you don't pass any of your favorite stores. Never go shopping without a list—shopping for clothes should be the same as shopping for food: only buy what you need. If you don't have a list, don't go to the mall. This will stop that drive-by shopping when you just "pop in" to see what's on sale. Make sure you're tracking your expenses, as this activity alone will keep you mindful of your spending.

Remember, too, that just because something is a bargain doesn't mean it shouldn't be put through the same rigorous test as would a larger purchase. Price and value are two vastly different things. Regardless of price, value is what you're looking for—things that bring real value to your life. Oh—and if the price is the best thing about an item, you don't need it. If you're desperate to buy something, stop and ask yourself: *Why am I so desperate to buy this thing?* What are you hoping buying this thing will do for you? Do you need this item or just want it? Does it help you to meet your goals and overall vision? What will you get rid of to make room for it in your home? If the answers to all these questions add up to "buy it" then walk out of the store and go home. Give yourself the gift of waiting forty-eight hours. If after waiting you still want the item, ask yourself the most important questions of all: *Will this item help me create the life I want? How am I going to pay for it? And what am I going not to spend money on in order to afford this?* If you can't afford it today, you can't buy it today. Simple (and as painful) as that. Even if it's free, leave it alone! You don't need it adding more clutter to your life.

Research has shown that "experiencers"—people who spend money on a great meal out or a concert, for example—are happier than those who spend their money on material goods such as clothes or jewelry. Don't forget: experiences allow you to spend quality time with family and friends, whereas buying another pair of jeans is a lonely endeavor. Also realize that "being a good shopper" is exactly what those stores, marketers, and ad campaigns want you to think about yourself. Be stronger than that!

Excuse #2: But I work hard—I deserve this.

In addition to the media and our friends leading us to believe we deserve a lot—the brand-new car, the flat-screen television, the latest fashions, the designer house, and so on—it's easy to convince *ourselves* that we deserve these things simply because we work hard. If you constantly put yourself dead last in your priorities and take care of everyone else first, it's quite natural to feel you deserve to be rewarded. And that reward can easily mean buying something when the best reward is giving yourself time and space to relax, recharge, and reengage with yourself and your family. When you're exhausted and craving a little time for just you, do you find yourself shopping and spending money? Do you feel entitled to buy anything you want when you feel you've gone beyond the call of duty as a caretaker? Does spending money seem like the only outlet to shouldering the stressful weight of managing a household and caring for your loved ones? Reality check: telling yourself that you deserve to spend money because it's finally time for *you* is not a solution. Nor is it a healthy means to take care of yourself. When you work hard, you should also work hard to recharge and relax without deepening your debt and financial troubles.

The Financial Impact: You Deserve Your Endless Debt

The problem with this excuse is that it tends to become a catch-all. People overuse this excuse to justify buying anything. And, of course, that's where the trouble comes in. If you were able to say "I'm loaded and therefore I can buy it," I'd have no problem with this one! Working hard can help you get out of debt more quickly but buying things just because you're working hard doesn't.

The Solution: Think about What You Deserve that Costs Nothing

Okay, so we all feel like we deserve *something*. But why does deserving something always have to be about money? Aren't the best things in life free? Don't you deserve to have great relationships, great kids, a great-working body, a great career, and so on? Working on these things doesn't require any money whatsoever!

What You Need to Do Today

Make a list of all the things you deserve because you've been working so hard. Now cross off all the things you think you deserve to buy. What is left over is what you really deserve and what will really make you happy. Whenever you feel like buying something to help you relieve the stress of working too hard, pull out the list and choose to do something that will make you happy instead. Give yourself the gift of the time you would have wasted shopping to do something more fulfilling. Go for that run or make cookies with your kids or call up an old friend and spend some quality time together on the phone or find fifteen minutes of alone time to recharge your emotional battery. When you reward yourself with the things in life that make you truly happy, they will come back to reward you time and time again in a way that your material possessions won't.

Excuse #3: But no one in my family is good with money— we've always been like that.

No one is born knowing how to deal with money, just as none of us knows how to ride a bike without some instruction and practice. Letting yourself believe that you're not—nor ever will be—good with money is the equivalent of sweeping the dirt under the rug. It's a total cop-out. It's simply an easy excuse for not owning your own problems. And for not taking responsibility.

The Financial Impact: Your Money Problems Deepen and Your Stress Builds

As we've said many times already, hiding behind your problems won't solve them, it only makes them worse. We all know what happens when we avoid something we shouldn't. It doesn't go away. It continues to build up and up and up. Meanwhile, we know it's there and sensing how big it's getting begins to seep into our subconscious and stir up a new source of ongoing stress and tension that we can't shake.

The Solution: Teach Yourself

Anyone can learn how to manage money well, and the knowledge to do so is freely accessible these days with the help of the internet, books, one of your smart friends, or a professional financial advisor. In addition to the tracking and other tools I'm giving you, check out resources online (see the box) that can help you to further customize a plan to your specific financial needs. There are numerous sites and programs available online and in books specifically geared to debt elimination and budget creation. These resources will take you step by step through the process of evaluating and dealing with your income and outflow. They will also give you invaluable lessons on managing money now and for the future.

RESOURCES TO CHECK OUT

The following authors are well-known for their debt, credit, and money strategies. I recommend reading their books and visiting their websites:

Suze Orman: www.suzeorman.com
David Bach: www.finishrich.com
Jean Chatzky: www.jeanchatzky.com
Dave Ramsey: www.daveramsey.com

The following personal finance websites offer budgeting guidelines and a wealth of tools:

http://money.cnn.com
http://moneycentral.msn.com
http://finance.yahoo.com

A note of caution here: While surfing the web, watch out for debt management and debt consolidation scams. They are everywhere. Just Google "debt" and you'll find thousands of entries, many of which can lead you down the wrong path. For help in finding qualified people who can truly help you get your credit in order and deal with your debt, start by contacting the National Foundation for Credit Counseling at www.nfcc.org (also http://debtadvice.org). You can also check out the Federal Trade Commission's website at www.ftc.gov for guidance and the Better Business Bureau (www.bbb.org) to check up on certain firms. Keep in mind that no one—*no one*, not even a nonprofit organization that comes with a five-star rating—can guarantee you a perfect turnaround or that your debt can be erased easily and effortlessly. Some services are legitimate; others are not. Do your homework and ask for referrals from friends or family members if you can. Beware of hidden fees, too. You may think that you're paying someone to take the burden of fixing your credit from you, but in reality, you're going to do most of the work and may have to cough up a lot of extra money to do it. Avoid anyone who calls him or herself a debt negotiator or credit repair company. Most of these are scams, and you won't get what you paid for.

What You Need to Do Today

Start learning today. Visit the library or pick up a book that teaches you basic finance principles, or sign up for a class at a local community college. If that's not your thing, find a friend that you trust who is good with finances and ask if you could get some tutoring. Feel empowered, not victimized—figure out how you can conquer that irrational and negative feeling that you're not good with finances.

Tracking your expenses and monitoring where and how you spend money is essential to understanding your financial situation. Another way to track expenses and monitor your cash flow is to use the cash-only envelope system of bill-paying. Based on your monthly expenditures, create a spending plan. First determine what bills will be paid by check or direct debit from your checking account, taking into account when they need to be paid—first of the month, middle of the month, or end of the month. Obviously, you can't pay for everything with cash. Pay your basic bills (rent/mortgage, utilities, phone, cable, water, etc.) and everything left over is what you have to spend for the month.

Every purchase you make after the bills are paid should be paid with cash only! This includes groceries, personal items, a trip to the mall, lunches, toiletries, household items, gasoline, and so on. Create separately labeled envelopes for the categories of cash-only expenses you have. For example, "household items," "personal care," "lunches," and so on. Then determine how much cash is allocated for these purchases. You will pay for these items using that set amount of cash from each envelope. This prevents you from spending more than the allocated amount when you're in the store. You cannot use credit cards, debit cards, checks, or store cards. If you run out of cash, you can't buy anything else.

Make only one visit to the ATM per week and only take what you need for that week. You can divide and allocate the money you have to spend in any way that makes you most comfortable. One way to do it is to give yourself daily envelopes for everyday things like food and groceries but weekly envelopes for sundries or transportation expenses and one monthly envelope to cover big-ticket items you had budgeted. If you've got a partner and children, you need to agree to a per-person allowance. Going on the cash-only system is an eye-opening experience that can reduce your overall expenses significantly. Try it for at least one month and see what happens!

Excuse #4: But I'm feeling guilty/sad/upset/angry (or even happy/ celebratory/excited)—buying something helps me feel better.

This excuse is a close cousin to the "I deserve it" one. Sometimes we let emotions get the better of us—and sometimes we let them get the best of our wallets. But think about it: What if you let emotions drive every decision you make? You'd soon find yourself in trouble because you can justify any purchase with any emotion—happiness, sadness, anger, stress, and so on. Emotions can make for irrational and stupid decisions. They also can give you a false sense of security and short-term pleasure that eventually turns into long-term struggle and strife.

The Financial Impact:

Buying while emotionally out of balance is sort of equivalent to driving while under the influence. You just don't make your best decisions and your reflexes are all off! This kind of buying—often called impulse buying—can lead to serious financial trouble (especially if there's a pattern of this kind of behavior). But you probably already knew that.

The Solution: Try to Keep Emotions Out of Your Buying Process

Take a very objective approach when you weigh the factors into whether or not you should buy something. Don't listen to the part of you that wants a reward and the quick-fix high. Like a sugar rush, it won't last . . . and the withdrawal will also draw from your financial security. Remember to ask yourself these questions: Do I need this? Why? What do I already own that is similar to this that I could use instead? How am I feeling? Why do I want to buy this thing? How did I feel when I bought the last thing I bought? Was it the same feeling that made me shop today? And how did I feel about that purchase when I got home? Stay focused on the rational side of buying; don't ask yourself whether or not a purchase will make you happy—ask whether it will serve a purpose that also feeds into your vision. In other words, think purpose, not pleasure.

What You Need to Do Today

Be prepared for bad (and good) days. What else comforts you on those days? Is it being with a good friend? Eating a chocolate bar? Going for a walk? Whatever it is, work hard at realizing that you're still in control (even when you don't feel like you are). Find healthy substitutes for impulse shopping and retail therapy. Commit today to choosing those activities over the mall the next time you get the urge to grab your purse and hit the stores.

Excuse #5: _____
(Fill in the blank with your unique excuse.)

Got another excuse I haven't covered related to money? Go ahead and write it down.

ASKING FOR HELP

I've mentioned this before but it's worth repeating: there's nothing wrong with reaching out for help to get a handle on your finances. A good financial planner can tell you the 1-2-3s of organizing your debt and then help you estimate how much to pay toward which bill every month so that you can start to save for your future. Although this will cost you a little bit of money, sometimes it's money well spent. The stress of having to take care of so many bills, formulate a realistic budget, and plan for your future while also taking into consideration the debts you have to service today can be daunting. Maybe you don't even know what it means to "live within your means" because you really don't know what your means are. Or you've been living on credit for so long that switching to living on income alone while servicing your debt and saving for the future has left you paralyzed by the thought of budgeting on your own. Maybe no one has ever explained how to create a budget, balance a checkbook, or use credit wisely.

A financial expert can make sense of your numbers and even take into consideration things like vacations, eating out, big-ticket items on your family's wish list, new clothes and furnishings, setting up an emergency fund, considering your retirement fund options, investing opportunities, and unexpected expenses in addition to your everyday living expenses—both today and in the future. You won't need to rely on this person forever. You may just need one or two appointments with an advisor to set up your system and get you going, then a few checkups once or twice a year as needed.

Don't panic about finding the "best plan." There is no single, foolproof remedy to managing your debt and planning for your future through savings. Your initial plan of action will change over time as your needs and circumstances change. Recommendations vary depending on which trusted advisor you listen to. Most personal financial planners would encourage you to set aside a predetermined amount every single month regardless of how much debt you're servicing, while others may claim that paying off outstanding debt should be your highest priority. Every situation is different, and a financial advisor can take your unique circumstances into consideration when formulating a personal plan. Also don't feel pressured to hire a financial advisor if it feels unnecessary or unrealistic due to cost issues. Do what feels appropriate for you. Taking responsibility for your financial life means researching your options and deciding on a course of action that makes best sense for you.

Regardless of whether or not you choose to work with someone, hold onto the vision of the life that you want as you work to create your life budget.

Dear Peter:
I was downsized [recently] when the corporation I worked for reorganized.

First, we pared down or eliminated any nonessential services to conserve cash—no more housekeeping help, fewer restaurant meals, and, thanks to a more relaxed dress code—

no more dry-cleaning bills! Lots of little expenses that were part of the "work ethic" but didn't add value to our lives used to add up to a large amount of outlay when we were working in the corporate world. Now scheduling is easier—no rushing to be ready for the housekeeper, my son is more responsible for his own items and involved in helping out, and we've found activities that we can enjoy at home without major expense.

I've always enjoyed gardening—but we have now dedicated more of the garden to edible crops—particularly the fresh herbs. By buying vegetables locally at the farmer's market, we found our grocery / eating-out expenses were smaller, and our eating was healthier. My husband has become interested in baking—he has become adept at "artisan" bread—so we have fresh baked hearty loaves at a fraction of the bakery cost.

It's been a one-step-back, several-steps-forward process, and I've learned to accept the downtime and pauses as a gift/opportunity rather than a roadblock. Slowing down the mental "hoop jumping" has allowed me to think about what I really enjoy doing—and what I don't. And then I can plan for the future and execute the plan.

Because we've become practiced at paring down time commitments, clutter, and financial expenditures, we have been more flexible in response to changes in the economy or whatever curve life throws at us.

MAKE SPECIFIC COMMITMENTS

By now you've completed several exercises on the money front. You've taken your financial audit. You've rethought your financial vision. You've reconsidered your wants and needs. And in doing so, you've begun planning for your future. Now I want you to focus specifically on which goals will help you reach your financial vision.

First, list the goals again here (it's okay if they've changed since the last time you did this exercise back on page 120). If you've modified your goals since starting this book, it's a good sign. It means that you're finally adjusting your vision to the confines of your resources, and reality. For this step, though, I want you to list just three financial goals—one that you can accomplish this year; one for next year; and one that's doable within five years. We're not going to worry about goals ten or more years from now. Sometimes, just focusing on the smaller, "nearby" goals can be more motivational and practical. With these goals under your belt, you'll then be able to work on those larger, longer-termed goals.

Financial goal for this year: _____

_____

Financial goal for next year: _____

_____

Financial goal within five years:

_____

To make these goals even more doable, let's attach a specific—and realistic—commitment to them:

One thing I can do differently every day to meet each of my financial goals is: _____
(Example: *Spend no more than five dollars on lunch and ideally prepare it from home.*)

One thing I can do differently every week to meet each of my financial goals is: _____

_____

One thing I can do differently every month to meet each of my financial goals is: _____

_____

Often, it just takes a single shift—a single commitment—to make a lasting, big positive impact. Bring this exercise to your next family meeting and share it. Encourage every member of your family to go through the same exercise. And then put all those little steps and goals into one chart and keep it somewhere very prominent to remind everyone of the commitments you've made to one another and to your future.

Where Is Everyone Prepared to Save?

Another activity you may choose to do with your family is to make a list of the little expenses you're willing to cut in order to help save each month. Each person in the family must commit to give up at least one thing that will make a measurable impact. Calculate how much money this will save your family each month, then deposit that total amount directly into a family savings account before you or your kids have a chance to spend it. This way you will have to stick to your savings commitment.

ACTIVITY: WHERE CAN I MAKE SOME SAVINGS?

Item	Cost	x number per month	Total
Restaurants / take-out / order-in			
Coffee shop routine			
Movies, magazines			
Weekday lunches			
New clothes and shoes			
Electronics			
Cosmetics			
DVDs / music / games			
Happy hour drinks / going out			
Travel			
Weekend splurges			
Other			

Total savings per month:

Own Up to Spending Eccentricities

I know one family that highly values Friday night dinners at a local restaurant, and I know another family where the mom gets a weekly massage and the kids each have a cell phone with unlimited minutes. These things bring joy to everyone, and are nonnegotiable expenses. But both families are committed to save in other areas of their lives in order to have these things without overextending their budgets.

Every household has spending contradictions and idiosyncrasies. Perhaps you appreciate fine wine but avoid fancy restaurants where the mark-up is outrageous. Or maybe you let your wallet run loose once in a while to satisfy your penchant for Swarovski crystal jewelry but you drive a ten-year-old car and have no intention of getting a new one soon. You may hunt for bargains and shop at big-box stores but don't think twice about paying high prices for organic food, premium gas, and first-class plane tickets. It's okay to have spending quirks, but only if you can balance your finances and save money before you treat yourself to these luxuries. If you're in a partnership, you should both be on board with your spending choices. Now is the time to talk to all your family members about what you as a family really need and what you can let go of in order to achieve financial relief and security. I'm guessing you'll be surprised when you actually examine your spending quirks that there are items that you can readily let go of if it means moving your family closer to the financial security you want.

Dear Peter:
Cutting back is a highly creative endeavor. When things feel a bit dreary here at the Villa of Reduced Circumstances, the restlessness that once drove me to shop can usually be satisfied by rearranging the furniture, shuffling accessories, or bring-

ing in a bouquet of flowers from the garden. It's a rare week where everything sits where it sat the previous week. I'm always cheered up by paint, often from the Oops bin (mis-tinted and sold for a few dollars). I glazed the walls of my workroom with a watered-down bottle of craft paint that cost 50 cents. I rethought my wardrobe and pulled out some accessories that had been tucked away so long they're back in style.

One thing I did miss was being able to make the sort of charitable donations I once did as a matter of routine. So now I look for other ways to pitch in. I give things away. I donate blood. If I go out for a meal, I try to do it when a local restaurant is hosting a fund-raiser for a charity I support. (Facebook is a great way to keep track of those events.)

I take care of anything I can't afford to replace. I retied the springs on my saggy sofa and sewed a slipcover from painter's drop cloths. I am religious about upkeep all around my house, making repairs before they become expensive. If I don't know how to do the job, someone on the internet does.

It's really all about attitude. Of course I miss travel, and worry that my dogs will get sick or my car will break down. But I'm learning to trust that I can handle it.

CUT, CUT, CUT

As with financial planning, a book about the secrets of cutting back could take up an entire shelf. Here are some basic tips to help you cut back that most families find doable. See how many of the following ideas you can subscribe to—starting today. Some of these tips are about basic necessities, but many relate to the things we've categorized as necessary when in reality they don't need to be.

Food Fitness

Healthy families are happier families. And there's no better place to support your family's health than with what you choose to eat. With half of all meals now eaten outside the home, we are spending more money than ever on fast food and restaurant meals. People are increasingly using credit cards to pay for fast food now that these restaurants are no longer cash-only. (Some have argued that there's even a link between the ability to use credit cards to pay for fast food and our obesity epidemic; a study of credit card use at McDonald's found that people spent 47 percent more when using credit instead of cash!) Don't forget about those elaborate buffet bars now in mainstream grocery stores that sell food by the pound and end up costing bundles of money—and calories. Even the least expensive restaurants cost more than preparing food at home and it's hard to control not just your wallet when you buy food outside the home but also the food's nutritional content. Two ways to save money and eat healthier: eat breakfast from your own kitchen and bring your lunch to work. It might take a little extra time in the morning but the benefits will far outweigh getting up fifteen minutes earlier. Breakfast does not have to be elaborate but if you eat at home instead of having that $3 latte and $2 muffin every day the savings can add up. Have your kids make their own lunches rather than tossing them lunch money. That way they'll pack what they want to eat and they'll start learning responsibility. And usually, when you make a meal at home or pack your own lunch, you will actually make and eat less than if you don't have control over your portions. If you don't know how to cook, it's easy to find simple recipes in magazines, cookbooks, and online. Start with simple dishes and involve your family—maybe one of them is a budding chef who would love to be involved with making meals.

When it comes to grocery shopping, healthy choices can sometimes cost more than junk food but the investment in your health will pay dividends in the long term. Junk food adversely affects your health and well-being and, ultimately, your ability to perform well at your job and your kids' ability to do their best at school. One thing you have to be careful of, though, when you shop is that you are eating what you are buying. It's all well and good to buy vegetables and fruit and healthy snacks but if you are just throwing them away every week because you never ate them, they aren't helping you and, in fact, you are actually throwing money away. Before you go shopping make a list of what meals you intend to make during the coming week, then make a list of what you will need to prepare them. Make a pact with the family: if we buy it, we're going to eat it. I've written a whole book on the connection between the weight in your home and the weight on your hips. Check out *Does This Clutter Make My Butt Look Fat?: An Easy Plan for Losing Weight and Living More* for detailed strategies and techniques for tackling this area.

Electronics

I am sorry, but if you are serious about saving money you do not need the just-off-the-assembly-line gadgets. Did you buy a first-generation iPad because you had to be the first on your block to own one? Do you have the next (better) flat-screen TV already in your sights? Does your teenager have the latest gaming system and digital camera? It is negligible how much, if at all, these expensive luxuries may improve your quality of life, but I question whether they improve it significantly enough to warrant the level of debt you can incur acquiring them. It's not a matter of life or death to be an early adopter. Electronics are highly disposable and as the technology accelerates, prices *decelerate*. Only buy new electronics if your old version is broken and only then after you've made sure replacing it is really necessary to your life. For instance, if you have four TVs and one breaks, do you really need a new one? Wouldn't you rather have that money in the bank and live with three TVs right now? And don't forget: make sure you know before you buy how you are going to pay for this new gadget and what you are giving up in order to afford to buy it. If you are honest with those answers, you may quickly realize that you don't need the latest and the greatest.

Home Improvements

Until you're happy with your financial situation, only do home improvements that are truly necessary. Repairs or replacements like a new roof or windows that will improve and protect your investment in your home are smart money. Avoid financing any renovations through your credit cards or equity lines, and stay within your means.

Maintaining your home is a necessity, decorating it is not. If you want to decorate or feel the need to go buy something new, look at what you already have. Can you move furniture around? Can you make a slipcover or paint? Get creative with what you own and you'll save money and have more fun than going broke buying a new couch because a magazine tells you the one you have is no longer ideal or fashionable.

Clothing

The vast majority of clothing we purchase is the result of impulse shopping. Stop doing it. You spend too much money on stuff you just don't need. You didn't get where you are—feeling like your life is cluttered and out of control—without bringing too much stuff into your home and your closets. Keep remembering that you really need very little to be happy and they don't sell happy at the store. Every time you have the instinct to shop for new clothes, go to your closet instead. What's in there that you haven't worn in a while (or ever)? Go shopping in your own closet: try things on, accessorize and pair pieces you don't usually wear together. Give yourself time to breathe and think of new outfits. You'll be surprised that all of a sudden you have enough with what you already own.

Children's Clothes and Toys

Examine the reasons you can't stop buying things for your kids. Maybe buying things for them makes you feel like a better parent. Maybe it gives you a sense of control. Maybe it makes you feel better about not having enough time with them. Maybe you buy things for your children in order to answer one of your own needs or to fulfill your own dreams. Or maybe you want your kids to be cool because you weren't. Perhaps the only reason you indulge your children is because you want to (temporarily, it turns out) silence the endless begging and pleading. Maybe you are caught in the idea that more is better and have a misguided sense that the more things you give your kids the more you love them. The same rules that apply to your own purchases go for anything you want to buy for your kids. Ask yourself: Do they need this? Do they actually want it (really, did you ask them)? Do they already have enough of whatever it is you want to buy them, or what they want you to buy them? (How many cute jeans can they have before they grow out of them? How many games?) Instead of continuing to spend your money, start giving them an allowance and teach them the value of money. Let them earn and save for what they want so that they learn early the value of things (and the ease with which money disappears). Teach them to ask the right question: "Is this thing something I really need? And will owning it enhance my life?"

Gifts

I'm all for gifts when they are useful or inspired or celebrate a major milestone, but not when they are given for the sake of giving. If you have the kind of relationship with your friends and family where they know what your financial situation is, then it is perfectly acceptable to send a thoughtful handwritten card for a birthday or holiday. It really is the thought that counts! If the holidays are an over-the-top gift exchange in your family, propose this year that only children receive gifts, or implement a secret Santa drawing, where each family member chooses a name out of a hat and gives only to that person. Don't be embarrassed or pressured into keeping up with the Joneses—especially if your family is the Joneses! These are the people who should have your back. You would do this for them and you have to trust that they will do it for you.

> Dear Peter:
>
> We have been going through some extremely tough times just the past few weeks. I've been staggered to discover just how many gift vouchers we had lying around the place! I found $250 worth of gift vouchers that can be used at the local grocery store and another $50 voucher for the movies.
>
> I also have a heap of things which I'm not using, which I planned to sell on eBay "one day," but it never seemed worth the hassle for any particular item, but now I think I'm going to create a lot of extra space in my home, and probably net a couple of thousand dollars by getting rid of it all.
>
> I was also forced to review the outgoings on our business. I managed to cut $12,000 per year from our ongoing running costs. So by going through this cash flow crisis, we've made our business "leaner and meaner" and equipped it better to return to profitability.
>
> It's still a painful experience, and not one that I thought I'd ever have. I'm definitely going to emerge from this experience with a more healthy business, solid friendships, and lots of lessons learned.

RIPPING OFF THE BAND-AID—FOR GOOD!

I can't finish this section without another nod to the shopping god. For many, many people in our consumer culture, recreational shopping has become an antidote for boredom or unhappiness. It's the Band-Aid we use to cover up those emotions we don't want to deal with. Not surprisingly, shopping is the primary hobby of many people I work with. These people don't get as much pleasure from the items purchased as they do from the shopping itself.

WHAT'S YOUR SHOPPING PERSONALITY?

The following questions will help you to identify what kind of a shopper you are. Complete the following statements (and be honest; write down what spontaneously pops into your mind as you read these leads):

I shop when: _____

Shopping makes me feel: _____

The place or store I spend most of my recreational shopping

time is: _____

When I buy on impulse, it's mostly goods in the following

category: _____

The things that I most buy that I don't really need are: _____

_____

I stop shopping when: _____

After a day of shopping I feel: _____

A few days after a shopping spree I feel: _____

Did any of your responses surprise you? Use what you learned so that every time you want to shop you stop first to examine your emotions and reasons for wanting to. With greater insights into what triggers your need to shop you can take greater control of your behavior and consciously intervene when that "I need to go shopping" voice starts chattering inside your head. Remember, pause before purchase. Talk yourself through every purchase, clearly distinguishing between a want and real need. Don't be fooled or swayed by the irrational, emotional part of you that wants a reward. The true reward is achieving the vision that awaits you when you learn to say no!

Once you've identified the triggers that compel you to shop, look for new activities to fill those needs. Try imposing a six-month moratorium on shopping. Start with one week, then build up to a month, then two until you reach the six-month mark. Every time you want to go shopping find something else to do. Pick up a book, or a rake, or the phone. Lie down on your floor and stretch. Run around the block. Grab a shopping bag and empty out a closet. Nothing except the bare essentials (food, cleaning supplies, toilet paper) comes into the house. Figure out what you might have spent every time you wanted to shop and instead put that money in the bank. It's a challenge, but not only will you see how few purchases you truly need, you'll jump-start savings.

SET BOUNDARIES

I've said that in your physical space, your relationships, your job and your family you need to set limits. The same is true for your money. If you don't honor and respect your relationship with your money, that relationship will eventually sour and, like the clutter in your home or a bad boyfriend, become overwhelming, suffocating, and even paralyzing.

The concept of a keeping to a budget is something that frightens and overwhelms many people but it shouldn't. A budget is a tool to help you manage your money, reach consensus on what is reasonable spending, and track the financial health of your family. Budgets are also ways in which we can set our boundaries around money—the rules that we set up for ourselves in order to maintain a semblance of control over how we spend and allocate our financial resources. Boundaries are what keep us focused and moving closer to our goals. I've already given you lots of examples of boundaries in this book, and you may have already come up with a few of your own. Examples include:

- Instilling the forty-eight-hour rule: don't buy until you've spent two days asking yourself why you need to buy this item and how you'll pay for it.
- Setting dollar limits above which you must discuss your purchases and get "approval" by all family members. For some the limit can be as low as $50. Discussing your nonessential purchases (i.e., items that have nothing to do with basic living expenses) should be part of your conversations with your family members.
- Sticking to cash and using credit cards only for emergencies.
- Keeping to the commandment: If you cannot afford to pay for an item in full today, then don't buy it.
- Considering old-fashioned layaway terms for buying items that you cannot pay for in full today but that you truly need.
- Setting aside a certain amount of money each month to put toward savings.
- Servicing your debt consistently by allocating a certain amount each month toward outstanding bills and credit card balances.

When it comes to money, you need to set boundaries that help you balance your needs and desires in the present with your needs and desires in the future. With clear boundaries, there are no unwelcome financial surprises and your financial situation is clearly laid out. This type of financial organization frees you from many of those nagging worries and concerns about the unknown.

Boundaries don't just exist for money-related issues. In your decluttered home, I ask you to set boundaries by keeping only the amount of stuff with which you can comfortably live the life you want to live. In relationships, those boundaries are more abstract and personal. At work, you need to establish boundaries that separate your work life and your home life. It's up to you to figure out which boundaries fit your life and choices, and establish them today with your family. Everyone's set of boundaries will be different. If, for example, your family has a tendency to spend money on eating out and buying the latest gadgets, then you'll need to establish very clear boundaries around those weak spots and ensure that everyone in the family is accountable for abiding by them. You can think of boundaries as an owner's manual or set of bylaws. When followed, they'll help you and your family be more efficient, goal oriented, and successful.

PERSONAL ACTION PLAN FOR YOUR FINANCES

Get clarity: Communicate with your partner about your shared vision for managing your finances. If you aren't both committed, you won't succeed. Set boundaries. Live *below* your means. Examine your reasons for spending money every single time you want to. Ask yourself the questions we've already gone over. And even if you are clear to proceed, still give yourself at least a forty-eight-hour cooling-off period before committing to a purchase. Only by changing your attitude about what you already own and what you need (not want or deserve) will you be able to stop buying more things, let go of the clutter, and find a financial balance that makes sense for the life you want.

Get real: Face fears. Owning up to your money troubles is the first step toward solving them. If you ignore debt, it gets worse fast. Overcome obstacles that prevent you from doing financial paperwork and bill-paying. Come clean with yourself and your partner about your money troubles and prepare to move forward together as team over your financial situation. Deal with your debt immediately. Commit time, even if it's only twenty minutes during which you research budgets and financial planning tools. Don't forget to celebrate successes. As you simplify your finances, you will feel more relaxed and secure. You work hard for your money. Enjoy knowing that you're making the most of it.

Get going: Make a commitment today to live in the present, but with a clear vision for your future. Make sure everything you do is helping you achieve that vision. And if you need just one thing to do today . . .

A task for today: Create a space for dealing with your finances and mail on a regular basis. And (well, this is two things, really) if you don't already have an emergency savings fund, set one up today.

7

The Home Audit: Your Stuff

When I pulled up to Jan and Rodney's modest two-story home in suburban Atlanta, I saw immediately that they were a hard-working couple who'd put a lot of energy and love into their home. From the tree-lined street their home looked welcoming, their lawn well-manicured, and I spotted a few freshly planted flowers under the front windows. A blue minivan was parked in the driveway. Colored chalk markings from the kids' hopscotch game were visible on the sidewalk, and a few children's toys were perched against the wall adjacent to the front door. I rang the bell.

To say Jan had her hands full was an understatement. As she welcomed me into her home, with her eighteen-month-old daughter, Claire, balanced on her hip, Jan was clearly showing signs of exhaustion and being overwhelmed. I could tell she felt a little embarrassed by the disarray that greeted me as I stepped across the threshold. The site was ghastly. "I'm sorry this place is such a mess," Jan said, "but this is why you're here. Help."

The front door opened into a living room that was littered with children's toys, used drinking glasses, and candy wrappers. A side table was covered with food crumbs and magazines. Catalogs were stacked on a couch, papers were stacked high on a small desk in a corner, and a video gaming system with all its cords and cartridges took up the central coffee table. There wasn't much room for anyone to sit and enjoy what could have been a beautiful and spacious family room. This disaster zone continued throughout the various rooms of the house. The kitchen was overrun with children's toys, unwashed dishes, and small appliances that looked like they had never been used yet were taking up most of the counter space. The table in the breakfast nook was almost buried by what appeared to be crafting materials for a school (or perhaps a home) project: glue, construction paper, colored pencils and markers, stacks of photos and magazines clippings, and books. Laundry—both clean and dirty—invaded the bedrooms, and I was surprised to find Jan and Rodney's bedroom decidedly worse off than their kids' rooms. Their closets bulged outward and under the bed lay more clothes (shrink-wrapped!) and boxes of shoes. File-type storage boxes containing paperwork lined the sides of one of the house's main hallways.

The tipping point came when I saw the garage and basement, both of which had become wall-to-wall storage units. I don't think another shoebox could have fit into the garage. Rodney, who owns a sports-themed pizzeria restaurant in town, had inherited his grandfather's baseball card collection and about one-third of the garage was jam-packed with boxes filled to the brim with old cards. They had once been confined to a public storage facility, but the family decided to move the cards home and save the monthly charges. Other signs of a bygone era were also visible everywhere: outdated computers and monitors, decades-old boxy televisions, rusted out bicycles, and boxes of cooking magazines dating back twenty years (Jan's collection, a relic of her days when she planned on being a chef). Jan rarely cooked elaborate meals now, and her dream of becoming a chef had been deferred for so long it seemed lost. The basement was a depository for old furniture, and untold numbers of boxes packed with worn-out clothes, books, and memorabilia.

If you were to pass Jan and Rodney on the street, you could not imagine that they lived in a house like this. Jan used to manage a flower shop but gave up her job to be a stay-at-home mom for a few years until her youngest was in school. They have three kids, the oldest of whom is a seven-year-old boy. Then there are the two girls, a five-year-old and the toddler. The irony of it all was that Jan admitted to being a clean freak before she had kids. And her husband ran a tight ship at work, keeping the restaurant and its kitchen spotless and tidy. To have a home so messy and cluttered was just not like them. Or was it? When I turned to the couple after my grand tour of their cluttered, messy, and disorganized home, they looked desperate. And sad.

I asked them when they thought it had begun to get so out of control. Jan said it was after her second child that things began to unfold. "There's been a parallel decline in our home with our income," she said. "Now we're suffocating. We have bills we can't pay. I can't afford to hire someone to help me keep this place clean." Rodney explained that his business had taken a bad turn and he was barely staying afloat. He had lines of credit maxed out, including an equity line of credit on the house that he had used to pay for business expenses. The couple had argued over whether Jan should go back to work, but they couldn't figure out how to they'd afford to pay for proper child care given Jan's projected income. They couldn't sell the house, either, because it had declined in value so much compared to what they owed.

They had exhausted their savings and for the last few months they'd had to rely on credit cards to pay for living expenses, and then they had suffered two big setbacks. The first was a $10,000 hit when their eldest child suffered appendicitis and their insurance coverage didn't foot the whole bill at the hospital. The second was that the previous winter the furnace unexpectedly gave out and they had to replace it. Now their debt, excluding their mortgage, exceeded $70,000 which was terrifying because they had never had unmanageable debt before this. They felt stuck, and sinking further with every passing day. Though they had given up the lease on one of their cars, it hadn't made much of a difference to their financial health. In fact, losing that car put more strain on the family because now Jan had to drive Rodney to work and the constant battle over car privileges exacerbated their frustration. Rodney fought his business's creditors every day now, and his makeshift home office where he tried to take care of his business's problems (to avoid scaring his employees at work), had tsunami written all over it. I personally didn't know how he could get anything done in that room.

The tension between Jan and Rodney became more and more evident to me the further I probed them about their situation. It was a story I had heard numerous times, just told a slightly different way. A short five years ago, when the economy was booming and they were a family of three, life was very different. They had savings. They could make annual contributions to their retirement accounts. They had minimal credit card debt, high credit scores, and copious offers for more credit in the mail on a daily basis. Rodney's business was going strong, too, and there was no need for Jan to contemplate work outside the home. They vacationed once a year, and never thought twice about purchases they made. Life was good. And then very quickly, it wasn't and they were not prepared.

IT'S NOT ABOUT THE STUFF

Jan and Rodney are not alone in their experience, and it wasn't one thing that caused their downturn. As with most Americans who wake up one day and suddenly wonder *what went wrong,* a constellation of events happened and the cumulative effects eventually accelerated that inevitable decline. Jan and Rodney never pictured themselves as the arguing type, but now they bickered about money constantly. Rodney wanted to put every single dime into rescuing his business and scolded Jan for continuing to shop as if they had the same income as before. Attempts to cut back on living expenses weren't helping all that much; meanwhile they were dealing with a 40 percent income loss. Something had to give.

If you know me, you know that all of the work I do has one common starting point. Clutter—no matter if it's in your home, your head, or your heart—is *anything* that gets between you and the life you want to be living. It's no different when we talk of financial health—clutter is anything that impedes you from achieving the life you want.

Dealing with any clutter, however, never starts with "the stuff." To make real progress and to achieve permanent, long-term change you have to start with the vision you have for the life you want. A simple, reasonable, considered, achievable vision that is the expression of what *you* want for *your* life. It's as simple and as profound as that. With this in mind I started with a simple question: What do you want *from* your home? As I expected, I heard the words "peace," "harmony," "balance," and "space." When Rodney added the word "wealth," I asked him to tell me what he meant by that. He said, "I want my home to be a source of wealth and security. It's far from that now. We owe more on everything in this house. It's all a sham. I'd rather live with a quarter of this stuff and have a bigger bank account than to live like I'm barely treading water and drowning in unpaid purchases."

Now Rodney was on to something. He was beginning to see that the stuff in his house wasn't getting him to that vision he had for his home—for his life. He also made a great point about the notion of wealth. Too often we think of wealth in terms of money, but it's also about health, success, and happiness. How can you be truly wealthy if you're not living the fulfilling life you want and feeling good about it? Where's the wealth in material possessions if you're not able to enjoy them and know that they bring you a sense of security? Owing the bank for a big house you cannot afford is not a sign of wealth. Owning a home outright, however, now that's security. Rodney was literally right on the money when he said that wealth meant something other than having things that were still being paid for with borrowed money.

When I asked Rodney to list the most important things in his life, his response was typical: family, health, being financially secure, having a successful business. When I pointed to specific objects crowding the spaces of his home, I asked him if they had any role whatsoever in his list of important things he'd just made. Does the mound of laundry make you feel healthy and secure? No. Do the boxes of old books, clothes, and memorabilia truly help your family today? No. How about those baseball cards collecting dust in the garage? This is where he hesitated, complaining that they weren't necessarily directly to his current life but that they *could* in the future. Not only did they hold sentimental value to him, but he could sell them and make money. My question, of course, was why didn't he contemplate doing that now to help his family get out of debt? Wouldn't that be helpful? Rodney squirmed. How could he sell his grandfather's beloved collection?

Helping Rodney understand the difference between his emotional connection to the baseball cards and his memory of his late grandfather became the starting point for dealing with all of his clutter. I forced him to come to terms with why he was holding onto these items that weren't adding any real value to his life and livelihood.

Dear Peter:
My family has been through a very rough economic period in the last five years or so, as I had a serious nerve injury, which led to unemployment, which led to depression. We have survived five years of pretty extreme hardship, but things are now finally starting to look up. For us the economic downturn doesn't mean much as we have been down for so long I can't imagine we could be worse off.

So now we talk about what we want from life and how to feel more connected to each other, and not get caught up in the "chase after stuff." In some ways we have a great head start as we have learned to live with much less. But still we have a house full of stuff. Maybe it works both ways. Have too much money, accumulate stuff. Not have enough money, accumulate cheaper stuff, and don't let it go through fear of that meaning a further slide into poverty.

I am happy with less in many ways, but in other areas I'm not. But I don't care we have a ten-year-old TV. I'd like some more nice clothes, but maybe that'll only happen when I throw out all those ill-fitting and old rags in my wardrobe?

WHY WE COLLECT

As I stated earlier, it's practically human nature to acquire things throughout our life, starting very early on. It's normal and natural and there's nothing wrong with that. Some things are given to us, some left to us, some we find, but most we purchase. Everything in your home is there with your permission—it's there because you are there. All the stuff in your house is there because you think it holds answers, evokes memories, contains a promise, or serves a purpose. Scratch the surface and I'm guessing you know all the stuff you've spent so much money and time collecting isn't necessarily bringing you closer to the life you want or fulfilling the expectations that you have. At one time you thought that the larger house, the shinier car, the more extensive wardrobe, the latest electronic items, and the newest clothes would transport you to a place of happiness and success. Now you're in a home surrounded by things and the cost to your life, relationships, and bank account isn't anywhere near the value of the goods. The reality of what you are living is exactly the opposite of what all those TV commercials and glossy magazine ads promised. Too much stuff creates a physical barrier between you and what's really important. Jan and Rodney knew this before I arrived, but it helped to have me there to confirm their feeling and to guide them through letting go and, more important, to help them recalibrate their "value scale."

VALUE SCALE QUIZ

Do you know the difference between value and cost?

What does "value" mean to you? Describe: _____

_____

What does "cost" mean to you? Describe: _____

_____

Does value always equal cost? Circle: yes or no.

If something costs $5, can the actual value be worth more or less than that? Circle: yes or no.

List the five most expensive purchases in your home:

1. _____

2. _____

3. _____

4. _____

5. _____

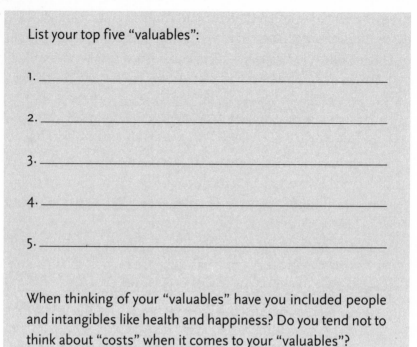

List your top five "valuables":

1. _____

2. _____

3. _____

4. _____

5. _____

When thinking of your "valuables" have you included people and intangibles like health and happiness? Do you tend not to think about "costs" when it comes to your "valuables"?

Value is what a thing is actually worth, and cost is what's on the price tag or what you're willing to pay. Both are expressed in monetary terms, but value and cost are also measured in terms of time, energy, and the intangible elements of a thing that either enhances the quality of our lives or not. When you pass a rack of clothes on sale in a store, you see a sweater that costs $19.99. But what is it really worth to you? What will that sweater bring to you and your life? What if it were $29.99? Would it be worth that much? Or is that cost too high? We are so focused on what things cost us, that we forget to ask if it's bringing value to our lives. And what is its real cost once it comes into your home? How much room is it taking up? If you buy the sweater for $19.99 but don't pay it off for three years because you've used a credit card, do you know how much that sweater really cost you in the end? About twice that amount, $37.98. And by then, three years later, you won't still be wearing it and may even have thrown it out or given it away! But you are still dealing with the credit card balance and the worries about paying your bills. Hence the need to recalibrate our value scale so that it's not just about the "face-value" cost of an item, but also about its real cost for us and our families and the value it would bring to our lives.

It also helps to keep in mind that something that you deem valuable may not actually be the thing that cost you the most to acquire or keep. In fact, it may not cost you anything at all in dollars and cents. We value our friendships and loved ones, for instance, but don't have to pay for them in cold hard cash. We value our health and ability to live productive lives but cannot put a price tag on those.

For most of the people I work with, this sense of unease with the things they own grows over time until it is almost overwhelming. This unease can be very sneaky and affects people on a subconscious level. At first, having a few too many things just makes them feel crowded and can make them cranky when they walk into a messy room. But then, as the clutter builds up something else happens. My clients describe feeling smothered by their stuff and are surprised by how emotional and physical their reaction is! They realize how much they hate the clutter-filled and disorganized spaces they have and lives they live and yet feel unable to change. They also hate not being able to have people over, feeling constantly stressed, and getting their monthly bank and credit card statements that confirm their out-of-control spending habits. They know that they own too much and yet they continue to buy things. They can see that their home is overrun but still they bring more stuff through the front door without ever removing anything from the house. The stuff wields amazing power—and yet they have every excuse under the sun for why they can't let any of it go.

As I combed through Jan and Rodney's home and started to target certain items, like those baseball cards and cooking magazines, the excuses started flowing.

SO WHAT'S YOUR EXCUSE?

I don't care who you are, when it comes to personal stuff I've heard every excuse in the universe. Here are the top two.

Excuse #1: But, it's too important to let go! It has sentimental and nostalgic value to me, and represents my family's history.

We hold onto our possessions because we believe they're important—to ourselves, to others, to our family, to our heirs, to our dreams, or to our own personal story. We may also have a great sense of entitlement to keep them for whatever reason. We may not need a certain possession at all anymore (and may never have) but we want it nevertheless.

If these items are supposedly so important, though, the question is how are you treating them? I have no sympathy for people who tell me something is important if it doesn't look like it from the way they are treating it. If the "important" item is buried in a box somewhere or gathering dust in a cupboard in the basement, how can it be important? What does "important" mean? How can you still need or even want it? If you really value and think you need to keep an item, then why don't you show it off as a way of honoring and respecting it? Either you value something or you don't. Either you have room for something or you don't. Either you truly need something or you don't.

This was the message I had to drill into Rodney when it came to those highly sentimental baseball cards. For all intents and purposes, they reflected—they *were*—his grandfather to him. And to do away with them was the equivalent of doing away with his grandfather. I had to prove to him that this "memory clutter" was in fact disrespecting the real memory. There was a better way to honor and celebrate his grandfather, and at the same time make the most out of the cards.

You're sentimental, emotional, and social. You value your family history as would anyone else. On the one hand, it's nice to be sentimental and to feel an emotional tie to things, but this can come with a cost. I've worked with families who haven't had visitors over for years because they're so embarrassed by the clutter. The cost of their stuff has robbed them of valuable relationships. And that is not a healthy equation.

The Financial Impact: You Lose Sight of What Value Really Means

Holding onto important items from the past is not a bad thing—unless remembering the past becomes more important than living your life today. Once emotions enter into the equation, any ability to dispassionately judge the value of an item is easily lost. Nostalgia can cloud perception of the true worth of an item. Is that old sewing machine truly valuable or is it really a broken piece of equipment that held special meaning for your mother and you feel obligated to keep it?

Memory clutter also entails recalling how much a certain item cost you and maybe even what it felt like to buy it. It's hard to part with things that were expensive, that cost you a long time to pay for, or that brought you so much joy—albeit fleeting—at the time of the purchase. You may no longer have any use for or need to keep a given item, but doing away with it after working so hard to acquire it seems impossible. This is when your ability to truly value that item becomes distorted by your emotions—both the emotions that you once had for the item when you decided to buy it, and the feelings you have now. If you are not fully *in* your life, it's impossible to make balanced decisions about memory clutter, financial clutter, or any area of your life.

The Solution: Focus on Honoring the Memory

When strong emotions are associated with an object the goal is to detach the memory and your current emotions from the physical object so you can focus on honoring the memory and let go of the object.

For example, rather than save a whole outfit or a threadbare quilt that holds tremendous sentimental value to you but which has no use today, cut a piece of the material and frame it next to a photo of the family member it reminds you of. If any words or stories help recall the memory, write them down and include them in the frame. Most of us have a box of little items that we don't know what to do with because aside from the memories tied to them, we don't really need or want them. They often include the knick-knacks that remind us of past events, trips, time periods, or our children's tender years. They can be hard to do away with because they are rich in nostalgic value. But you can still honor these items by displaying them in a box or shadow frame or, as is the case with flat children's artwork, a ready-made frame. Over time, they may not seem so significant to you and you can replace them with newer items. Your celebration of these items and the honor and respect you show them will result in them having new meaning and value to you today. They didn't mean much when they were stuffed in a drawer, but now they add real value to your life because they properly memorialize your personal history.

What You Need to Do Today

With memory clutter you need to work to separate the memory and your emotions from the object so you can view its value from an objective standpoint. Why do you need to keep the object when you have the memory? Every time you go on vacation do you come home with a camera full of photos, three new sweatshirts, and other paraphernalia that then gets stuck in a drawer? When you look at those objects now, the broken lei, the baseball hat with the shark, the miniature Westminster Abbey, do you think about how much you spent on them? Do you remember why you bought them in the first place? Do you need to look at a particular item to remember your son's first swim in the ocean or your daughter meeting Mickey Mouse? No, you don't. Understand that when everything is important nothing is important. Pick out one or two items that have the strongest positive memory for you. Display those items with honor and respect. And let the rest go.

Excuse #2: But, I might need it one day.
I could sell it and make a lot of money!

Some of us are afraid of the mysteries that the future holds. Life can take some pretty scary turns. Who knows what could happen? You want to be prepared. At the back of your mind it may be more than just the possible future need for an item that compels you to hold onto it. Perhaps you see some financial potential in items also, and tell yourself that one day you'll be able to sell these things and make a profit. One day. The problem is that one day seems never to come and that perfect time to sell the items just never seems to arrive. Whether it's the pull of the past or the anticipation of some possible future, these excuses can hold a tremendous power over you. This is what I saw in Rodney, too. Aside from the emotions he felt toward his grandfather's baseball cards, the future-profit possibility alone that he saw in the collection also controlled his behavior and prevented him from doing anything with them.

The future is important and preparing for the future is a sensible and important thing to do. But you have to consider the quality of your life right now and strike a balance between the life you are living today and multitude of possible paths your life may take in the future. The "we might need it one day" is often a cover-up for our fears about the future, especially given the recent economic fallout. None of us has any idea what will happen, how bad the economy can get, or where we'll be in the future, and the best we can do today to try and control that great big (and scary) unknown is to hold onto our stuff. What's more, you may add to that stuff by buying *more* stuff "just in case" you need those things next year when things are *really* bad. During those end-of-season sales, are you tempted to stock up on a new set of winter clothes or another pair of sandals just in case you won't be able to buy more next year?

What this behavior really does to us is prevent us from living our lives fully today. In the now. In the present. Clutter has this ability to keep us out of the present, and deep in debt. Wanting to be prepared for the future is a wonderful thing, but not when it so preoccupies us that we forget that the only time we really have is the now. And think about all that money, space, energy, and time that you spend now trying to prepare for futures that may never come to fruition. Neither you nor I (nor your stuff!) can control what tomorrow brings. When I urge you to get rid of the "I might need it one day" things, I'm encouraging you to let go of those things that limit your present and get in the way of your future. Make room for what's really important: all your hopes and dreams and the life you deserve today.

Dear Peter:

I'm not in debt and generally do live within my means, but in the last couple of weeks I haven't been careful with my finances. I was surprised to see my bank account so low this morning. The problem is I've been buying too much just in case things go downhill. You've done so much to help me get a handle on my cluttered house (and mind) and I would hate to undo this because of my fears that we won't be able to get the basics. I've had several people say to me the same thing in the past few weeks: "Are you stocking up on things?" At this point I'm confused if I'm being prudent or obsessive and not trusting that life will provide in the future? I really don't want fear to run my life, but it seems I'm not immune to it. Do you think this crisis can create more clutter chaos?

The Financial Impact: The Opportunity Cost of Lost Space, Time, and Energy

Preparing for the future by getting rid of credit card debt, saving money for education and retirement, and taking care of your health is a sound and sensible practice. It's when those preparations are not sensible and they start to destroy the life you have today that there's a serious problem. Throwing good space after badly spent money only compounds the problem. Look at what you've surrounded yourself with. How much money have you thrown away on things you "need" for the future that you'll never actually use because that imagined future never comes? How much are these items actually worth to-day? Could you sell them online and use the cash elsewhere? Why do these items hold so much power over you? How can they really "save" you in the future? If you're not using these items today, why do you think they'll suddenly be useful later? Can't you see that their cost is far greater than the money you've spent? These items are costing you in unusable space, in stress, and very possibly they are costing you every month in credit card bills.

The Solution: Live in the Now and Attach Present Value to Things

Accept reality. Come to terms with the diminished value of the stuff you've spent money on. Find out how much these items could sell for today. Don't fool yourself into thinking items will retain or in-crease in value just because you think you'll use them someday. Be-ware of adding too much sentimental value to things. Look at your stuff objectively, as would a potential buyer. If an item holds some power over you that you just can't shake, ask yourself: Is this thing really key to my vision? How can I turn the energy I have wrapped up in this item into an everyday source of power that I can carry with me to achieve more monumental goals?

Have an honest conversation with family members about stuff they think they "might need one day." Does your son really want that old coffee maker in the basement when he goes to college in three years? Will your daughter really ever wear all those wool sweaters stored in your old trunk? Probably not, but someone will. Get into the habit of regularly giving away or selling what you don't need and don't use. Any money you make can go into your future fund, which you definitely *will* use someday.

What You Need to Do Today

Immediately stop buying for the future. And give your clutter this test: If you bought something or have kept something because "one day you might need it," look at that item and say to yourself, "Today is the day I've been waiting for." Now ask yourself, "Do I need that item right now, today?" If the answer is no give it away, sell it, or throw it away. If the answer is yes, take the item out, find a place for it. Go to your calendar and pick a date at least one month from now and write down the name of the item you just deemed necessary. When that day arrives if you haven't used this item, you never will. Let it go!

THE COST OF YOUR DEBT

Being overwhelmed by stuff is a physical and emotional hurdle and I hope you're starting to see the benefits of conquering all kinds of clutter. Those benefits are huge, much bigger than the effort it will take to clean up your life. One of the main reasons I am so ada-mant about clutter is that I see how the space it occupies in peoples' lives seriously hinders their personal growth and development. It crushes them physically and spiritually. No matter how you look at it, holding on to your clutter is simply not worth it!

As you read this chapter, you may be subconsciously perform-ing your own personal audit along the way. You might have begun to really see the clutter that surrounds you, and you may have heard a few of your favorite excuses spring from that cluttered brain of yours. What if I were knocking at your door right this instant? What would you want to hide? How will you explain yourself when I point out x, y, and z? If I asked you to show me your financial statements, would they belie what I'm actually seeing in your home? Do you appear rich but feel and live poor? And what if I said you could live rich and feel rich from this day forward? What if I could take away your fears and trepidations about money and replace them with a sense of power, self-confidence, and peace of mind?

Remember the image of a baby gripping onto things? We all want to wrap our hands around what we believe will bring us more happiness, more health, and more wealth. The pathway to those goals, however, involves a little bit of letting go. It calls for a little blind faith in relinquishing what you *think* is important for a much greater good. And a much bigger outcome. Just as a baby must pick himself up and let go in order to walk for the first time, so, too, must you take a similar risk. I promise that you will reap so many rewards beyond just the immediate ones of having more physical space and fewer bills to pay. The money you used to spend on things can be freed for loftier goals and dreams—a child's college tuition, a small business, a loan or debt payoff, a cooking class to reignite an old goal, or anything you have on your vision list for the life you'd like to be living.

No matter what your religious beliefs are, each of us is called to be the best person we can be. We can't be our best when we are embroiled in stuff and debt. We not only lose sight of our goals and dreams, but we also lose sight of ourselves. It's time to get that clarity back—to stand tall as we did when we took our first steps in the world.

Close your eyes and think again about the vision you have for your home that I asked you to formulate at the beginning of this book. What did you see? What do you want from your home and its various rooms? Forget for a moment how everything looks today and stay with that image. Close your eyes if you have to and mentally walk through your house from the front door through every room imagining it as you'd like it to be. Be sure to include every space, including the attic, basement, or garage if appropriate. Then peek into the closets and hidden spaces of your ideal home. What emotions does your bedroom evoke? Does your kitchen make you want to cook? Does your dining room inspire you to host a dinner party? Don't forget the rooms and places typically occupied by others in your family, such as your kids' bedrooms or a spouse's home office.

If a room has been sabotaged by someone else, imagine owning that room yourself and having the luxury of doing whatever you want with that space. I once worked with a couple who stored a friend's woodworking equipment and tools in their garage. They took up half of the garage and were covered in a thick layer of dust. For nearly five years, the couple couldn't use the space as they wanted. They hadn't been able to park their cars in the garage, and the kids were banished from the area because of the risk of injury. When I told them that, intentionally or otherwise, their friend had been taking advantage of their generosity and that it was in their hands to bring this situation to an end, they agreed. And they took action, telling the friend that they needed the equipment out within a month. When he at first resisted, they made it clear that they intended to sell it in four weeks unless he picked it up. Great strength comes with a clearly articulated vision. This strength of purpose and clear focus on creating a space that reflects your vision can be yours, just as it was for this couple.

As you mentally move through your home, think about how you want each room to function and make you feel, as well as how you think others would benefit most from using the room. For example, how would you want your dinner guests to feel about your dining and living room? What do you want from your master bathroom? What do you need from your master bathroom? A spa-like experience? How about when you open your refrigerator door? Do you see a cornucopia of fresh, delicious food? Does your kitchen nourish your family? What do you like most about it? What do you like least?

Have fun with this exercise, even if you know that a gaping hole exists between what you imagine and what's currently there. You may notice that you begin to smile as you let your imagination run free here. This positive emotional response can be incredibly rewarding, motivating, and helpful to you in the next step. Hold on to that emotion and remember it. You'll want to call it back when negative emotions begin to surface later on. My goal here is for you to see how you could be living, and make identifying the areas you need to work on all the more easy. Chances are you've had blinders on for quite some time, so keeping this vision in your mental margins as you proceed to this next step will serve as a guiding light.

For some people, just imagining the rooms and the items they contain is hard. It may help to walk through your house room by room and take a physical inventory with a pen and paper. I took readers through such an exercise in *It's All Too Much: An Easy Plan for Living a Richer Life with Less Stuff.* If you choose to do this, aim to accomplish two tasks: (1) map out the specific vision you have for each room, and (2) take stock of what it looks like and how it functions for you today. Not only should you describe the individual vision you have for each room, but also specify its primary function and then record the items in that space that block you from the vision you have for the room. Here's the rule: anything that does not belong in the room, that does not help create your vision for that space or serve a specific purpose in that particular room simply does not belong in the space.

That Clutter Is Costing Real Dollars

It's easy to put a dollar figure on the cost of professionally stored clutter, but what about the clutter you keep at home? How much is *that* costing you? I'm not just referring to the financial cost. I'm also talking about what it's costing you emotionally. The emotional cost may exceed the dollar cost.

Try going through one room and make a quick estimate of the cost of what you're not using. For example, look in your bedroom and consider the cost of unworn clothes and shoes, unread books, unworn jewelry, or unused makeup. Consider the unused toys in your den or child's bedroom. If any particular item you come across tugs at your heart or makes you emotional, then consider that an added cost. Add up the cost of the items—I'm guessing that some of those clothes still have the tags on them so it won't be that hard— and write down the amount. Is it big? How much of that are you still paying off? This simple exercise should give you a rough estimate of the cost of the clutter in your home.

I once worked with a woman named Laura who had inherited her late mother's upright piano, which stood awkwardly in the corner of her living room where it looked out of place and was never used. Laura couldn't fathom getting rid of this family heirloom, though it brought back mixed feelings of her strained relationship with her mother (and of her years hopelessly struggling to learn how to play the piano). She wasn't quite sure if the piano was a symbol of joy or sorrow, but she wouldn't let it go. Whether it brought back good memories or bad, she felt it was her duty to keep it.

I asked Laura if she had any particularly fond memory relating to the piano and her mother and she instantly looked at ease. She said there were photos of her mother during her mother's prime years as a pianist that she cherished, and one photo in particular taken of the two of them at the piano when Laura was just a toddler admiring her mom's playing. Where were these photos? Why weren't they on display? Laura admitted that she kept them in a box in the basement, and never found the time to do anything appropriate with them. I told her that the piano was a poor substitute for the photos that captured the real memory and joy. It was time to do away with the piano, which was just clouding the good memories and blocking Laura from celebrating her mother in a way that highlighted the good times and honored their relationship. The cost of that piano in Laura's house was huge. It took up physical space, but even more it took up emotional space. It was impossible for Laura to put a dollar figure on the cost of keeping that piano but she paid the emotional cost again and again every time she saw the piano.

Another assessment you can do is to work out how much each square foot of your home is worth and then see how much of that space is unused due to clutter. Simply take the current value of your home (make a rough estimate; you're not trying to come up with the exact selling figure for real estate purposes so just obtain the general ballpark figure), and determine how much each square foot is worth.

Value of your home ÷ Square footage of your home = Value of each square foot

_____ ÷ _____ = _____

So, if you live in a $250,000 home and it's 2,500 square feet, then each square foot is worth $100.

The value of each square foot of my home is: _____

Now let's calculate how much of your home's space is occupied by things you don't use. Walk around your home and make a rough calculation of how many square feet are unusable because of the clutter. Don't forget the basement, closets, and garage!

The number of square feet in my home
that are occupied by things I don't use: _____

Now let's find out how much that wasted square footage is worth:

Value of square footage × Square feet occupied
by things you don't use = Value of unusable space

_____ × _____ = _____

Are you surprised at the value of the space you're giving up to things you don't use? Is it a big waste of space? A colossal waste of money for space that is lost to you and your family? Every month when you pay your mortgage company, a decent chunk of that money is paying for storage in your own home.

Now let's do this once more but this time go through and write down what everything in each room is worth. (You did a similar exercise in chapter 5, page 125; if you skipped that assignment, then now's the time to complete it—adding to your list items that you haven't actually paid for in full yet.) Mark which items have been totally paid for. And then write down how much you still owe on the other items. For example, let's say you have a big-screen TV that you bought for $2,000 when it first came out because you had to have it for the Super Bowl three years ago. Did you put it on your credit card? Have you paid the card off or are you carrying a balance every month? Think about it: if you are carrying a balance, some part of the balance you pay every month is that TV you bought three years ago. If that TV breaks, you are still paying it off even if you replace it. And then you'll be paying for both the broken TV and its replace-ment! Really look around your house and figure out exactly what you own and what you still owe money on. Was anything worth the worry and stress of those monthly bills?

SORTING THROUGH AND SIZING UP

I routinely meet people who have homes so filled to the brim with stuff that they easily have tens of thousands of dollars worth of pur-chases they rarely, if ever, use. Sadly, even when they try to sell most of that stuff they make far less than what they paid for it. Clutter's ability to steal your financial security is real. Almost without excep-tion wherever there is a clutter problem there is a financial problem. In all likelihood, you've accumulated stuff that cost you tens of thou-sands of dollars. Every item you purchase that you don't need or can't pay for robs you of money that could have gone to pay for much more important things in the grand scheme of your family's life, such as excellent health insurance, a college tuition fund, a business investment, or just a big emergency fund to have on hand for the what-ifs. For this reason, the *opportunity cost* of your stuff is sky high. Because you could have used the money elsewhere (and for more important goals), you lose a potential gain. It can be hard to quantify how much all this stuff has cost you in terms of time, energy, stress, sleeplessness, cleaning, storage costs, upkeep, arguments, and so on. But think about it for a second: your home should be the antidote to stress. If it's a source of anxiety and unrelenting upkeep due to its contents and chaos then something is out of balance.

Contrary to what you might think, the art of decluttering your physical spaces can be looked at from the same perspective as the art of shopping. That's right: it turns out that the part of you that controls your shopping behavior is the same part of you that will help you to climb out from under the rubble of your stuff and know what to do with it all. Let me explain.

One of the more complex human behaviors is decision making. Thanks to our highly developed brains, we have an amazing capacity to think critically and examine a situation from all angles before coming to a conclusion. This advanced processing of information is used every day in the things we do, including shopping. How many times have you stood over a table of clothes on sale and considered all the reasons why you should—or should not—try something on or make a purchase? When you see an advertisement on television for a huge sale at your local department store, the neurons in your brain start firing off. You begin to contemplate whether or not you should go and when; you begin to imagine what you might find, what you could look for, what you need (which is probably a want and not a true necessity), and you may even begin to make elaborate plans for the outing.

Underneath all that rational analyzing, however, is a more primitive area of the brain that simply wants to be satisfied. When faced with the decision to buy or not, to spend or save, this primitive area wants to be rewarded and can override our rational brain's anti-purchase reasoning.

The mental process we go through when we are buying things is the same one we can use when we are deciding what to do with the stuff we already own. Just as you now do when you shop, the goal here is to be conscious of the line between your true wants and needs, and then rationally focus on what will fill your needs.

When you took inventory of the rooms in your home, did you have a hard time figuring out what to keep and what to get let go? Did you get emotional at any time, perhaps because of a certain item's memory? The memories we attach to our possessions can be very powerful so work hard to separate the memory from the value of the actual item so that you can make the correct decision about its true place in your life. As you were taking inventory of what you own, did you simultaneously consider the vision you have for each room? After this exercise, do you think and feel differently about what you own, what you owe, and what you've chosen to fill your home and life with?

When you're ready to focus on the physical clutter that fills your home, map out how you'll address it all room by room. I suggest you start with the room that has the least amount of things that you're prepared to discard and then work your way up to the more cluttered rooms that may take you more time and thought to tackle.

Dealing with All that Extra Stuff in Your Home

There are only two things you need to do with the items that you want to let go:

1. Move them to their proper place if they were in rooms where they didn't belong.
2. Remove them from your home and your life.

Be careful if you move anything from one room to another. Before doing so, ask yourself: Does this fulfill a specific purpose in this room? Has it been used in the last twelve months? Am I keeping this just to keep it and am I fooling myself into believing this is a necessity? Is it worth the space it's taking up in my house? If you cannot come up with a specific reason for keeping an item, it's time to say goodbye. For example, moving your kids' high chair (ahem, it's an antique now that the kids are all grown up) from your dining room to your kitchen is not a good idea. Moving a stack of DVDs from the living room to your family room is a good idea—if there's adequate room for them. Moving a box of old books from your den to your garage or home office is not a good idea.

Dealing with Mixed Emotions

Watch out for those "collectibles." There's a superfine line between collectible and clutter. It's very easy to have an exaggerated sense of what something is worth—not only because you have attached memories to the item but because you remember what you paid for it and you hope it will be worth twice or three times that some day. It might. But it very probably might not. Stop making excuses for your collectibles. If you're in financial trouble, expanding your collection is not an option. Don't hold on to anything that doesn't add to the vision of the life you want or that adds to your debt. It's better to collect money, space, time, and energy than any single item. A true collectible is something that can be displayed in a way that honors the item, enhances your relationships, and contributes to the life you want to live.

By the same token, things we deem to have sentimental value can also cause problems when deep down we know that they no longer serve any practical purpose, and have cost us more than we can afford, but we just can't let them go. Don't forget; when clutter is sentimental, you need to figure out how to disconnect the memory from the item and how to preserve that memory in way that honors and respects it. By doing this, you can effectively take the power away from the object and liberate yourself from its heart-tugging clutches.

Remember Laura and her late mother's upright piano gathering dust and bringing unwelcome memories in her living room? Laura finally took back the power locked up in that piano by getting rid of it. She celebrated her mom's memory by showcasing the favorite photos of the two of them together.

I once worked with a man, Jeffrey, who stored his father's elaborate military memorabilia in an extra bedroom that had become a giant storage room. No one but he was allowed to enter this room and his wife grew increasingly furious that the space was "wasted" on all this stuff that meant nothing to her. When their friends or family members came to visit, the couple had to ask them to get a room at a local hotel because there wasn't anywhere for them to sleep. The other extra bedroom had been turned into a home office and was wall-to-wall filled with stuff. Its futon could barely be seen amid the piles of storage boxes, old paperwork, and knickknacks.

Taking Jeffrey through the process of reframing his feelings about his father's military memorabilia took some time. I asked him if this room made him happy, and after a long pause to think about it, he said no, and then added that he was surprised by that response. "Then why do you keep this room the way it is?" I probed. "I don't know. I guess to keep the memory close," he said.

I eventually got Jeffrey to realize that getting rid of this room's stuff didn't mean removing the memory of his dad or of his dad's military experience. Just as I had with Laura, I helped Jeffrey choose those items that represented his best memories of his dad and preserve those by allocating a section of one wall in this room to display them. It turned out that among all these things that filled this room, the item Jeffrey cherished most was his dad's Purple Heart, which had been stored in a box in the top drawer of his desk in the *other* room. We made a display case for that award and then surrounded it with all the items that reminded Jeffrey of his father, including photos and small pieces of fabric from his dad's uniforms. It took up just a few square feet of wall space and once it was up everything else in the room took on far less meaning for Jeffrey. He managed to detach himself from the other objects and began to sell what he could online and got rid of everything that was left over. Opening up that much space made us realize that the room could be best used as the home office, and that the other room currently serving as the home office could become a guest bedroom. After Jeffrey had gone through the experience of purging his father's clutter to preserve and celebrate his real memory, it was much easier for him to take that wisdom and experience and apply it to removing the clutter in the home office and only bring over the essentials to the new one.

Dear Peter:

I was laid off [a couple of months ago] and since then I've taken your ten-minutes-a-day advice to heart. It's made me realize if I started small I wouldn't be paralyzed by the daunting task of cleaning one entire messy space.

As I started cleaning up, I also realized how much of a compulsive spender I am. I think under the guise of needing teacher gifts and buying things on sale all year to have Christmas ready ahead of time I had accumulated way too much. Now that I don't have a job I can start giving away all of these things I have accumulated and get real about my spending.

I have always worked since I was fifteen, so this has been unusual for me to have time to myself. I pulled my son from daycare to save on spending while I am not working. It has made me a little less effective, but I'm taking the ten-minute victories over junk to heart. I'm not bitter about the work situation. I think this time is a blessing.

RESPECT THE IN/OUT RULE

Don't add to your clutter by "replacing" older items with newer ones but not doing away with the old. I should hope by now that you are no longer buying anything just to buy it, and if you do need to replace or update something in your home, then make sure to get rid of the old. No matter how big your home is, if you keep bringing things in but never take things out, one day you'll look around and wonder why it is that you have totally run out of space. One for one; it's very simple. From now on, for everything that comes into your home, something must go. The thing that goes must either be the same type as the new item or take up the same amount of room. You buy a new outfit; you get rid of an old outfit. You buy a new computer, you donate the old one. Don't talk yourself into storing it for "future use" or "just in case" "or because I spent a fortune for it." If you have spent money on something, then treat that item with respect. Work to keep it in good condition. Honor it because you brought it into your home and your life expecting it to make your life better, and plan to use it for a long time. If something breaks and can't be repaired, then you have to discard it, no matter what it cost. But if something "isn't right" anymore then figure out how to make it right, without spending a fortune to replace it. Be honest with yourself and your surroundings. Respect the limits that your physical space places on you. Just as every time you make a purchase you have to take the time to consider what you are going to give up to pay for it, you also have to consider what you are going to get rid of to make room for it.

Part of this new plan must include every single family member in your household because clutter of all kinds doesn't usually go away on its own or from a single person's effort. You all have to work together to achieve your vision. This is how Jan and Rodney—the couple I described earlier in this chapter—eventually took control of their clutter, too. Once each of them addressed their emotional ties with their individual stuff, they were able to work together as a team to sever those superficial connections and make room for what really mattered: preserving the memories wherever possible, separating what they truly needed from what was now useless and of no value to them, and creating new space for items that could contribute to their shared vision as a family. By the time I left their home, they could approach their stuff from a dramatically different perspective and come to measure happiness in a whole new light.

8

Change the Way You and Your Family Measure Happiness

IT'S EASY TO FIND OUR WAY INTO DEBT and be deluged under the weight of too much stuff, but it's not so easy to simply throw the situation into reverse and navigate our way out. A clear vision and established limits are key first steps in solving financial problems, but then comes the hard decisions. Can you create a home that centers on time together? And can you be happy doing that without the latest gadgets, new furniture, *or even in a smaller space?* Do you have the courage to make new choices for you and your family? Choices that reflect a commitment to the quality of your relationships rather than the quantity of your stuff? You know my answer to that is a resounding yes.

As I've been telling you from the beginning of this book, the quantity of our stuff can no longer be considered the measure of our success. It is the quality of our relationships and the state of our well-being that leads to deeper personal happiness. The rat race of owning more and having more doesn't just ruin your credit rating and cause clutter. It distracts you from concentrating on the important things in your life: healthy happy relationships with your family and friends—and most important, yourself.

You need to stop constantly comparing yourself to some fictional ideal that you believe other people are achieving. Remember, appearances are very deceiving. Those neighbors with so much that you so much admire may well be drowning in the same amount or even more debt than you. The paycheck of your co-worker is probably not as big as you think, and all the expensive things you've bought because they were supposed to fulfill you haven't changed your life one bit. You need to start chasing the inner peace that comes from not having to deal with, service, and maintain a level of debt that pulls you away from the life you want. Debt creates selfishness. You can't concentrate on what's really important if you're in debt and constantly thinking about it. How can you truly reach your ideal life if you keep spending all your time buying into what companies and marketers tell you is ideal and not giving yourself the time to work on what will really enrich you?

You can't live your best life in a cluttered, messy, disorganized space. I don't care what anyone says—it's just not possible. Similarly, you can't live your best life when you're in a place that is cluttered with worry about debt or financial uncertainty. That constant fear erodes all peace and calm from any life. Once you declutter and organize your life, everything takes on a different focus. The stuff is no longer important. And with less stuff you are more able to build the life you want. You'll be able to make the final leap and live in a space of comfort and tranquility, being able to embrace the emotional aspects of being truly happy and being truly content with what you have. Such a life will contain less in volume but more in meaning than your current situation. Imagine if you could free up the time and energy you currently devote to acquiring things and then worrying about what you have and what you owe and instead have that time to do the things that truly enhance your life. Imagine how different your life would be.

Now that you have the results you've collected from your audits, it's time to make a real and practical life plan. Much like a financial planner helps you set up and achieve short- and long-term financial goals, you're going to do the same thing and set up short- and long-term goals for the physical, financial, and even emotional and spiritual aspects of your life. The ultimate goal is to achieve balance in your life by way of the following:

- **Shifting your vision so it's more in line with your realities—and your family's collective vision:** This entails modifying your vision so it's not a far-flung fantasy more suitable for another life (where you have infinite space, time, energy, and money). Your vision for your life should be a reasonable goal that you can reach with concrete, doable steps that you can start today. Your vision can stretch your potential, but it should respect your access to resources, your financial reality, and the finite factors of your time and energy.
- **Shifting the way you and your family think about your stuff:** Once you move away from falsely thinking that more stuff creates more of what you want, you can appreciate the value of less. When you acquire less stuff you will actually get more of what you really want—more money, greater security, peace of mind, more time, more energy, and deeper relationships.
- **Shifting the way you and your family measure happiness:** Ask anyone what makes them truly happy, and they won't say their stuff. They will point to their friends and family members; they will mention their health, children, and their passions. You probably did that when you asked yourself the same question in the first part of this book. Happiness is not derived from material possessions. It's derived from our relationships, and our overall health and wellness. Once you learn to detach happiness from acquiring and owning things you can focus on what truly makes you happy—and actually achieve that.

And if you can make these three shifts, then you can realize your fullest potential and live up to every vision you've set for yourself and your family.

So how do you make these shifts? You've probably already begun to make some changes yourself as you've been reading but to make the changes lasting, you have to involve everyone you live with. I've titled this next step "Change the Way You and Your Family Measure Happiness" for a reason. If you share space, possessions, finances, and feelings with your family, then you won't succeed in redefining your life if they're not part of the process. If you haven't done so already, from this point forward you must include your family members in your plans for creating the life you want—for them and for you! You can change all you want, but unless you have the full support of your family you won't be able to fully realize the changes you seek. This inclusion involves more than just telling your family members what they need to do to help you deal with your audits. This step is about helping your family members understand how important it is for them to make the same mental shifts that you are committed to making. It's about stepping up to the plate as a parent and role model. It's about seriously talking to your partner and kids about money and opening the lines of communication as early and as often as possible. It's about truly creating a family plan. It is about making choices and understanding why you're making those choices. It includes the tough talk about what might need to be given up and what's to be gained from making those choices. Changing the way your family measures happiness doesn't start with bossing them around to pick up their rooms and take the garbage out; it begins with the basics of talking about what you all want, where you all stand, and where you'd all like to go.

If part of you is feeling dazed and confused by everything you've done so far, then let this chapter settle down all those anxious feelings, including the ones you have about bringing your other family members into the loop. We'll take it slow. You have no problem communicating with your significant other or children about everyday things, but when it comes to big issues like status, material possessions, entitlements, and finances, it's often a completely different story. So let's be sure you've got your entire family on board, which will make any unfinished business you have in fully decluttering, getting organized, and defining a family vision for the future a form of group therapy. You can only transform yourself and your life if the people in your life are part of the change.

> Dear Peter:
> My husband and I have had to deal with facing a layoff several times. He was laid off four times in six years. At one point I was also unemployed. We decided he would go back for his master's degree and we actually used my severance package to pay for his tuition! I just had our third child and we definitely learned to appreciate the "free" things in life. It may sound cheesy, but we were happier. We truly enjoyed everything we did and didn't take anything for granted. Less really is more and sometimes you are forced to realize that! It was a great lesson for us!

BE UNITED: MAKE IT A TEAM EFFORT!

I find it amazing that couples rarely talk about their financial goals or shared financial vision before getting married or living together. Money issues usually only come up when there is a problem so it's no wonder that fighting about money is the number one relationship problem.

Psychologists tell us that when couples fight about money, it's not really about money. It's about what the money represents—power and control. This is the same reason why fighting over spending money on things is not about the things. It's about what those things represent. If one person pays all the bills, handles all the banking, and dictates what the weekly and monthly budgets are, then, of course, the other partner is going to feel left out and powerless. That partner may, in fact, *overspend* in order to compensate for the lack of power. I see this all the time among couples where the man fills the traditional role of bringing home most of the income and handling all the finances, while the wife spends beyond the family's resources, finding her source of power and meaning in the mall. She uses shopping as a Band-Aid for the problems in her relationship and the imbalanced relationship she and her spouse have when it comes to money matters.

In another scenario I encounter a lot, the husband intentionally keeps the wife and, consequently, the children, in the dark about their financial situation. Oddly enough, this is his way of "protecting" them from bad or unsettling news. The husband thinks it's better to be ignorant than to be worried. Meanwhile, the wife and kids have no idea where the financial boundaries are, or they resent the limits placed on them by the husband because they cannot put those limits into any concrete perspective. If they don't know how much money is actually coming and going, how can they honor the family budget and feel good about how they deal with money? They can't. Power struggles ensue. Kids especially get angry when they feel they are being denied things that they really "need" and that they believe they are entitled to.

There's a fine line between leadership and dictatorship, and between authoritarian parenting ("Everything I say goes and that's it!") and authoritative parenting, which respects a child's self-control and decision making within firm guidelines and in a warm and loving environment. Open, honest communication and trust between parents and children and between partners is the only way to deal well with money issues and to set agreed upon budgets and boundaries.

No matter who takes charge of handling most of the bills and budgets, you have to have a collective vision for the financial life you want to live together. There's nothing wrong with one person taking the lead on managing the finances and paying the bills so long as everyone who is affected by those financial decisions agrees to the process, has a say in matters and understands the basic parameters of the budget. As a team, you have to decide what to spend money on, how much to save, how you'd like to be living in five and ten years—

together. Make a commitment to each other by taking the following steps and working together as a team to declutter your financial life so you can fully enjoy what's important to both of you. Once the kids are old enough to understand basic concepts about money and finances (which is sooner than most people think, around the age of five as they head off to kindergarten), then the children must also participate in this ongoing conversation. They may not necessarily be able to add and subtract in order to understand basic budgeting concepts and the value of a dollar, but they should start to understand that they can't always be given everything they ask for. You can certainly have private conversations about money with your spouse, but I recommend getting the kids involved as much—and as soon—as possible. A family that agrees on controlling spending and budgeting together is a family with shared goals and priorities and a strong bond. Below I'll cover some tips for how to get on the same page as your partner, and then I'll talk specifically about getting the kids involved.

Communication

One reality I must address right off the bat here is this: you may *still* be reading this book in a vacuum, totally disconnected from your family. You may even feel unable to broach this subject matter with your significant other. You may be excited to make the changes I'm recommending but have no idea how to engage your family because you are afraid of everyone's reactions to making those changes.

It's also possible that every person who lives in your home is aware of the problems but you are unable to come together and face them. Maybe you've even tried to initiate change in the past, only to fail because no one could agree on a shared vision or a shared plan of action. It may be unrealistic to think we can perfectly sync our visions even with the people we love and live with, but to move forward you must figure out a way to find common ground and incorporate everyone's vision. I find that often the greatest challenge is not so much in finding the ideal intersection of all visions, but in just getting that conversation started!

Realize that you're a team and that the most successful teams, whether we're talking sports or relationships, are ones where there is a lot of open communication and real trust. Plan a time when you can sit down and talk face to face, heart to heart without any distractions or interruptions. It's critical for all family members to have an opportunity to define their vision and to speak openly about the life they want and the things they want to surround themselves with. Of course I'm including children here, but it will be most helpful to start the discussion first with your partner. This way you will both have an understanding and a shared vision when you open the conversation up to your children. Have your partner go through the same exercises that you did in the previous sections, or, better still, go through them again as a team, exchanging ideas on what each of you has discovered along the way. How do your visions meet up? How do they differ? Where can they be modified to satisfy both people's needs? Are there any nonnegotiables to discuss? How can you make it work in the interests of all parties? How does your partner see utilizing your home's space, and all the stuff in it? Who is responsible for bringing most of the stuff into your home? Talk about that and how to change that impulse. Address the feelings you both have about need versus want and how money and owning things makes you feel. What does looking at your finances together do for your relationship? When you look at your finances together make sure you come from a place of neutrality. It is no one person's fault; you are where you are and acknowledge that together. The focus here is to move past where you both are to where you want to be. Did you find anything you didn't expect or that seemed to sting your relationship?

People's feelings about money can be complicated. It is very common for some people to feel intimidated, embarrassed by their lack of knowledge and skills in this arena, or even downright terrified by everything about money. Coming from this place of fear and anxiety can make for difficult conversations. A person who feels less competent, less involved, and less empowered may seem argumentative, resistant, and difficult to negotiate with. Have patience. Listen. The sooner you begin to have these conversations and keep having them frequently, the sooner you can all arrive at a common understanding of the situation facing you and what needs to be done.

I recommend that you make time every week or month to reconvene with your partner and see how you're doing. Be accountable for each other's vision. Sit down together, check your progress, and reevaluate your plan. Pay bills together, go through the mail, check on changing trends in your spending and talk about your goals, expectations, and fears as a family. It may help to define your goals in different categories:

- **Their goals:** have a clear understanding of your partner's goals, which may be different from yours. What vision is your partner working toward and which goals are you making him or her accountable for today?
- **My goals:** your partner should have a clear understanding of *your* goals, and how they play into your larger vision. Encourage your partner to hold you accountable for your own goals, and to help you rethink these goals in the context of your family's resources and basic practicality.
- **Our goals:** Make sure that you are not only on parallel tracks but that your goals dovetail with each other and that they are also contributing to the shared goals and vision you have for your family.
- **The family's goals:** spend time discussing your family's goals, and how each of your sets of goals adds to the family's overall plan. Do any of your individual goals take away from the family goals? If you have children, do you know what their goals are? Does any part of your children's goals demand your attention and support as parents? Do your children know what the family goals are and how they can participate in making them real?

The more detailed you can get in defining and elaborating on your sets of goals here, the clearer the steps you'll be able to take toward your vision. It's like laying down the bricks to your own yellow brick road. Wherever appropriate, these goals should also be incorporated into your family's budget. Your budget needn't be static—it can be dynamic and change as your family's needs and financial circumstances change. And if you haven't established a family budget yet, then make *that* your first goal!

Having the initial conversation about your goals with your partner may not feel like you're walking down any yellow brick road. It may, in fact, feel like you're walking into a swampy morass of old issues and thorny subjects that resurface and threaten to overwhelm you. This is especially true if you find yourself at serious odds with your partner's goals, and his or her ideas about how to use money are vastly different from your own. So what do you do? The impasse can be too big to overcome on your own, even if you have the best intentions.

Sometimes you may not have the knowledge or the skills to work out your issues yourselves or even contemplate doing a budget together. Or, there may be too much anger and tension that has built up over the years and you both find it impossible to put all that past history and behavior aside. That's when you know you need to seek professional help. As I noted earlier, don't hesitate to bring in a financial counselor if you feel it would be helpful and worth the money. Specifically, a trained financial planner with a background in psychology who specializes in helping individuals explore the emotional, practical, and spiritual aspects of their relationship with money can often help you to navigate not just the logistics of budgeting and saving, but also to get past the struggle of negotiating opposing viewpoints and arriving at common ground. A professional can also equip you with the right words to say to your children so your kids are more receptive to changes in the household. These professionals see people with problems like yours every day. They have the training, neutrality, and expertise when it comes to these situations. Their sole interest is in helping you succeed.

Dear Peter:

I wanted to share what my husband and I are going through. When we got married a few years ago I didn't know that he had $27,000 in credit card debt. I was raised by my grandparents, who didn't have much and taught me to pay what you owe before you spend on things you can really do without. When I found out my first thought was to run out the door and never look back. But after talking with my husband and my dad I decided to stay and help him out of this mess. It hasn't been easy. There have been a lot of sleepless nights. I have to really rein in my husband's spending, which can be difficult. We haven't been on a vacation since we got married.

To get him out of this mess he has given me full ownership of his business. I've never had so much responsibility before. It scares me to death at times.

The good news is that we just paid off two more of his credit cards this week. He started out with seven credit cards; now we're down to two. It's been long and hard, and yes, it most definitely put a strain on our marriage at times. I know there is still a ways to go, but hopefully we will get there.

Coaxing the Kids

When was the last time your kids asked you for money? Did you just give it to them without asking what it was for, or without them having to earn it? I'm not here to lecture you about how to raise your kids or tell you how you should allocate money to them, but many of the problems I see in families struggling to makes ends meet and dig themselves out from under too much stuff are rooted in the great divide between how the parents think about money and how their children do.

It's natural to give children money when they are still too young to perform any significant chores around the house in exchange for an allowance. But too often this habit of simply handing over money for nothing—or paying for whatever your child wants with a credit card—continues long past the point at which they should have gained a foundation in the rules of money. Not just general rules of money, such as where it comes from and how it relates to debt and credit in the world at large, but more important, how money functions within the context of your family's needs and constraints.

Do your children know what the family's unique "rules of money" are? Do they know exactly how your family makes money and how your family's basic necessities like food and shelter factor into the allocation of that money? It's taboo to announce how much you make to others, but for some reason parents feel it's also taboo to share with their kids the finer details of their financial profile. I believe this is a shame, one of the biggest mistakes parents make today. So not only do the vast majority of children grow up without a working knowledge about money from a practical and, might I add, life-sustaining standpoint, but they also are clueless as to how they specifically factor into their own family's money equation.

Try a simple exercise now. If you're single, do this yourself. If you're in a relationship, sit down with your partner. Make a list of five money rules that make sense for your family:

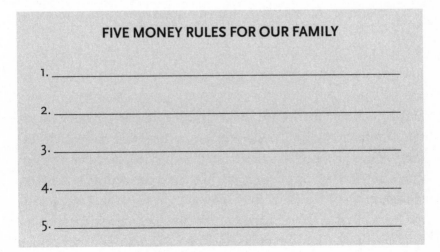

FIVE MONEY RULES FOR OUR FAMILY

1. _____

2. _____

3. _____

4. _____

5. _____

How easy was this exercise? Did you encounter any surprises or resistance? How regularly do you or you and your partner (and children) follow these rules? If you have kids, do they know these rules and adhere to them?

If a thirteen-year-old has no concept of what $350 means for the family's finances because all he cares about is getting his new gaming system, how can he even begin to reframe that want? How can he prioritize his short-term want of the game with his long-term goal of college if he doesn't understand the family money rules? He can't. And the aggravation and frustration that he feels when Mom and Dad don't get him what he wants can put tremendous strain on a family, until parents give in. The strain then becomes both emotional and financial, and destructive to the entire family. In some families, this cycle carries on into the child's adulthood, as parents continue to support their children's unrealistic wants and needs. On one level, it's gracious and also very empowering for parents to support their kids for as long as they can, but on another level, enabling their children to remain dependent has the effect of squashing their full development into independent and financially stable adults. Without understanding money and having a way to balance their wants and needs within their resources, they are doomed to repeat the financial mistakes you've made, and may even make more serious mistakes that you could never afford to fix for them.

Turn Off the Tap, Turn On the Truth

I marvel at how many kids grow up today thinking money comes from a hole in the wall. I shouldn't be surprised because that's exactly where kids see money coming from! Imagine what it's like watching from an early age as your mom or dad routinely drive up to a box beside a building, press a few buttons, and voilà, out comes money. Unless a child is taught about the realities of money and finance, it's easy for him or her to grow up thinking money comes from ATMs just like water comes from a tap. How and when do children learn to distinguish between an ATM and a water faucet? In many families, kids learn far too late—long after their parents have indulged them and heightened not only their sense of entitlement but their expectations. And this, I'm sorry to say, sets those families up for continual discord and conflict. The road to harmony and mutual agreement among family members (and siblings) can be arduous, a battlefield rife with meltdowns and power struggles.

Too often parents don't include their children in discussions about money and finances because they want to "protect" them from that "awful" and "scary" subject area that's better handled by the "grown-ups." Is it? Like anything else, children learn about money—what it's for, how to save it, how to use it responsibly, and where it comes from (not growing on trees or from a hole in the wall!)—by parental example. Avoiding the subject means your children will never learn and will grow up financially unskilled, believing that money is scary, and better handled by someone else. Is that the lesson you want them to learn?

Unless you introduce your children to the subject of money and teach them basics as they mature, they will never be able to balance their understanding of what they want with what is financially possible. The media exists to sell us stuff and it will succeed in programming your children into thinking they deserve everything and anything and that they actually need everything and anything. Does this sound familiar? You, as a parent and role model, must counteract this programming with an equal amount of knowledge and insight so that your kids learn to respect the limitations of all your precious resources: money, time, energy, and space.

Learning to handle and manage money responsibly is a skill like any other, and it is learned through education and practice. Kids need to be taught this skill because without it they are simply not prepared for the financial realities that they will face in life. If your parents kept you in the dark about money for much of your youth, or never taught you the basics of money management, don't you think that has partly contributed to your current problems? And wouldn't you want to avoid repeating the pattern in the next generation?

I can understand the other angle to the argument: you want your kids to have it better than you did. But why does having it better always come down to money and stuff? Having it better doesn't mean having children who are self-indulgent, selfish, or imbued with a sense of entitlement. What lessons are being taught if you give your kids everything they want and ask for? When children learn to equate love with receiving more or being given something, what kind of adults do they become? Most of us can remember the first time we actually bought something we wanted with our own money—money we earned doing chores, babysitting, or completing a certain job. Remember how good that felt to *earn* money and then decide what to spend it on? It felt good because you had worked hard for that money and it was *yours*.

Dear Peter:

At the end of my maternity leave last year, my husband took two months off. We spent that time in a motor home with only the essentials and our three kids. We traveled in Canada and the U.S. and realized how very little we needed to entertain ourselves and the kids. It took only twenty minutes to clean up our living quarters and an hour to do all of our laundry, leaving plenty of time for us to spend together, investigating our surroundings or playing games.

We have yet to transform our current lives to meet these standards, but strive to attain this simplicity. Upon returning from our trip, we purged a lot of stuff from our house and have a great deal more to do. We feel like we have redefined the meaning of our quality of life and identified what is truly important to us—experiences and time with our family, not stuff.

We can't forget the power of earning money on our happiness, sense of self-worth, and confidence. When money is just handed to us without having earned it, it doesn't mean anything. It's easier to squander someone else's money because there is no risk involved and there is no connection between that money and you. This partly explains the stories of people who strike it rich in the lottery, squander their money, and end up broke. Among the most famous of those is Evelyn Adams, who won the lottery *twice* in the 1980s and went from winning $5.4 million to living in a trailer. She wasn't able to say no when people asked her for handouts, and she also lost a bit to the slot machines in Atlantic City. The late William "Bud" Post, who died in 2006, collected $16.2 million in 1988, and eventually Bud lived on Social Security and food stamps. He called his win a "nightmare" and had to declare bankruptcy after falling into $1 million in debt. In 1993, a Missouri woman won $18 million, but eight years later she had filed for bankruptcy with only $700 left in two bank accounts and no cash.

I'll give you one more: In the early 1990s, one southeastern family hit a $4.2 million jackpot and, like the others, gave in to repeated requests from family and friends to help them pay off debts. They also bought a bigger house. Eleven years later, the couple divorced, sold the house, and split the meager proceeds. The husband had to move in with his kids, and the life insurance they had bought was cashed in. Indeed, luck is fleeting, and so is money unless you've got a handle on it. Experts who study these scenarios suggest that winners who get into trouble fail to address their emotional connection to the new money they've been handed. In addition to shouldering the new weight of the taxes and logistics of managing that money, they also have to bear the heavy burdens brought on by their family members and friends.

So the bottom line here that I'm trying to get across to you is that you need to stop just giving money to your kids. Instead, invite them into your family's conversation about money as early as possible. I understand that it can be tough to deal with the stress of your kids' needs to keep up with their friends and the trends, but the benefits of setting limits and living within realistic means will set them up for a lifetime of dealing with money in a healthy way.

Just like those lottery winners, you will be bombarded with requests for money from your kids. This won't ease up until they understand their own role in the family's financial picture. In the same way that you are working to curb your own spending, don't squander your family's money—and your children's future—by letting them have whatever they want. Break the association between spending and happiness, between love and receiving more, and between the acquisition of stuff and self-fulfillment.

When you let your children participate in the family's financial conversation and contribute to the solution you'll be surprised by how quickly they catch on and develop a healthy relationship with money. Don't underestimate your children. If you ask your kids to cut back on their own before it gets to be too much, they may consider the task a welcoming challenge and rise to the occasion. They will appreciate the fact you've let them into your "big, scary" world and included them in your planning.

Keep in mind, too, that one of the best things you can give your kids is actually free: your time. When you have more free time to spend playing and connecting with your children, everyone benefits. There's no replacement for spending quality time with your kids to bond and get to know them better, especially as they grow older and it's not so easy to stay attuned to what's going on in their lives and what they are thinking and feeling. There are an untold number of ways to spend time with them that don't cost you a penny! You could play games, make cleaning up a room in the house a team effort, visit a local park and throw a football around, have a BBQ in the backyard, or cook a meal together and eat around the table sharing stories. It doesn't take a lot of effort to come up with dozens of ideas for entertaining one another without spending a dime and enjoying each other's company.

HAVE REGULAR FAMILY MEETINGS

It goes without saying that just as you would schedule routine meetings with your partner or spouse, it helps to conduct regular family meetings as a group. These can be in addition to your partner meetings, or, if it works out for your family (and depending on the age of your children), family meetings may be the only meetings you need. It's essential, though, that parents come to the family meeting together with any serious differences hashed out already so they can talk with their children as a pair of like-minded coaches rather than using the time to hammer out their differences in front of the kids.

I know one family that makes the first Wednesday of the month their family meeting night. They cook a meal together, with the kids taking the lead and mom and dad assisting, then gather around the dining room table to catch up with each other and discuss any issue affecting the family. School vacations, household responsibilities, upcoming events and especially the family's finances are always on the agenda. In fact, mom actually writes up an agenda to make sure they cover everything—anyone can add to it—and takes notes so there's a way to review past goals at future meetings. Some of the agenda items related to finances include:

- Looking at the family's current financial position: savings, debt, chief assets, main expenses, and so on.
- Going around the table to share thoughts on current wants and needs: small- versus big-ticket items are discussed in relation to the budget.
- Reviewing past financial goals: Have they been met? Have they changed? Are they still realistic? What needs to happen in order for them to be achieved?
- Upcoming expenses: If it's getting close to the holidays or a birthday, the family talks about how to incorporate extra expenses into the budget.

- Long-term view: What needs to happen in order for long-term financial goals to be met? Though paying for college tuition or a car for your teen can be years away, it's good to consider these goals now and keep them in mind. They can help put other expenses into perspective. For example, if your son really wants a car on his sixteenth birthday, then buying a new entertainment system for his bedroom when he's thirteen may not be a priority. Instead of spending the money now for short-term gain, could he find an alternative to the new system and instead put that money into a college fund?

Every family will have its own rhythm in these meetings. Don't be afraid to explain to your children everything in terms of your financial position. Explain to them how you and your spouse devised the budget and what it means for the overall spending habits of the family. Be open about how their needs are part of the budget. Revise the tips I gave you when you did your financial audit and set boundaries that every family member must honor. Show them your checkbook and explain what it means, how it's used, and why you need to balance it each month. Explain the meaning of your different bank accounts, how they're used and how interest accumulates. The more meetings and conversations you have, the more they will understand the financial life of your household, the more likely that they'll understand where money comes from and where it goes every month. And they will start to grasp that the supply of money is not endless and needs to be constantly monitored and overseen if you want to stay on top of it.

Financially responsible kids are created, not born. It's your job as a parent to educate and inform them about money and financial responsibility.

Dear Peter:

Last year, I had my very own "financial meltdown," in which the stress of carrying my current level of "stuff" nearly drove me to a breakdown. I reassessed my entire way of balancing what I want, what I need, and what I'm willing to spend time working to pay for. Here are the changes in lifestyle and consuming that I've made:

- Moved into a small cottage with a dear friend. Savings: $700 a month.
- Turned in my leased car and bought a bottom-of-the-line Toyota Yaris (almost 40 mpg). Savings: $600 a month.
- Put myself on a Starbucks limit of once a week. Savings: $60–100 a month.
- Eat out inexpensively maybe twice a month. Savings: $200 a month.
- Shop in thrift stores, where I get just the things I really need and pay $2.99 or less. Savings: who knows?
- Buy pretty much only what I need for maintaining the house and running my business.

I don't miss spending money at all—in fact I get joy from seeing how little I can spend throughout a day. I buy only what will bring me continued joy and get me closer to what matters most to me.

What a huge relief! And what fun I'm having *not* spending money! I'm less stressed about work, have more time to enjoy my home, pets, and roommate, and most of all feel the tremendous lifting of stress, which frankly robbed me of any enjoyment of the "things" I was accumulating!

EXPECT CONFLICT

Okay, so I don't expect all of these meetings—especially the first few—to be conflict free. Expect some degree of surprise, confusion, and even resistance or resentment in this process. Change is tough, especially when habits have become ingrained and your family is used to acting less than responsibly. I have frequently found that although people may share a common living space and love for each other, their individual ideas or visions and expectations can vary enormously. Those differences will also change over time as people go through different stages and children grow older.

When I met Karen and Mike and helped them initiate their first family meeting, I knew that their experience was one shared by millions of other parents. By the time they waved the white flag in surrender, they were not only overrun by debt, but they were overrun by their children's expectations. Karen and Mike had three children, an eight-year-old girl and two older boys (a thirteen-year-old and a bona fide fifteen-year-old teenager who played the part well). One look at these kids arranged around the table and it was evident that they were not willing participants in the conversation. Their arms were folded tightly across their chests and all three of them were clearly angry. When it came time to discuss the cutbacks that needed to happen and what each person would have to give up in order to get the family back on track, the whining started immediately:

"But that's not fair!"
"I don't want to."
"No, I won't do it."
"You've got to be kidding me. No way!"
"Yeah, right. Whatever."
"I don't care. This is stupid."
"I hate you!"

Some of the whining turned into tears and the older son got up and left the table at one point in a huff. I had coached the parents beforehand so they would be equipped to deal with the situation. I made sure that Karen and Mike established where they stood at the start, and that they had their shared vision clearly mapped out. When the children began to get upset, I advised that Karen and Mike reiterate why the family needed to be making these changes. Coming from a place of love, they detailed their basic premise for the family, reminding their kids that they loved them deeply and that the point of all this was to make life better for everyone both now and in the future. Sure, it would require some compromise and sacrifice, but the end goal would outweigh the temporary discomfort. Karen and Mike also assured their children that nothing about the meeting was meant as a personal attack or a ploy to gain more control over their lives. This was new territory and Karen and Mike were very worried about what the overall reaction would be. However, when faced with this honesty and sense of seriousness, the kids softened somewhat. The first step was, and always is, the hardest. This was about including the children in the family's decision making so that the greater goals of each member could be met. This was about addressing each and every person's needs and honoring those needs as best as possible with the reality of their financial means. As a family they were in financial trouble and needed to do something *now* to address it—as a family!

If this approach is new in your household, expect things to be tough or frightening or emotional at first. Over time, though, including everyone in these discussions can only build family bonds and strengthen relationships. Establishing ground rules at the start of meetings is a good idea. Sometimes emotions, even anger, can rise in the heat of the moment and things can get difficult or uncomfortable. This is when mom and dad need to calm everyone down and steer the conversation back to those ground rules so that communication continues. One of the most important ground rules is to listen even if you're not hearing what you want to hear. Everyone's opinion should be regarded seriously. What is important to you may seem "dumb" to your teenager. And vice versa. You have to find a way to talk about your differences in the context of your family's financial reality or you won't get anywhere. Try not to play the blame game, either. When you find yourself using words such as "yours" and "mine," try and replace them with "ours." Though each of you will have your unique vision and contribution to the family goals, you need to see the family's financial position as a shared entity. It's an "ours."

As a family, once you create a budget, review your net worth in relation to your debt, figure out where you can cut back and pay bills, there will be fewer and fewer arguments. No one will be left in the dark feeling insecure and powerless. Remember, this is about coaching every family member through the process of making those shifts—of changing the way they measure happiness. Think of your open conversations about money as the vehicle through which you will make those shifts and move your family from a place of fear, debt, and ignorance to one of power, fulfillment, and enrichment.

Dear Peter:
As a result of all our free time and lack of extra money, we've been spending more time with each other as a family. We find ourselves doing more things that do not require payment like visiting parks, our free local zoo here, going for walks, swimming at the indoor pool, playing card games, and daring each other to do household tasks better or quicker!

We've learned a completely new way of living. We're also learning to make money from home by selling unwanted items online. It's been phenomenally successful, as so many people are buying things used due to the economy these days. All in all, we've become closer and are living cheaper.

TAKE THE SEVEN-DAY CHALLENGE

Need somewhere to get started in bringing your family together? Can't fathom having that first family meeting because you've never had one before and feel disconnected from everyone? If families are not connected, it's tough to have a shared vision, to feel like you're communicating, or to solve problems in a shared way that makes everyone feel valued and heard. With busy modern families this is truer than ever. I see it every day and I've come to realize that this lack of connectedness is a huge factor in creating unreal expectations, our sense of entitlement, and our misplaced sense of the value of money and things.

Recently I've become identified with the *Stripped Down Challenge,* which was featured on an episode of the *Oprah Winfrey Show.* The purpose of the challenge was to address this lack of connectedness in a typical American family and to help families everywhere that are extremely overwhelmed, disorganized, and out of touch with one another. By stripping people of things that keep them disconnected from others, such as computers and televisions, they are forced to reconnect and discover the value in authentic human interaction! The particular family that I worked with on the *Oprah Winfrey Show* was not an anomaly, for I hear from or see countless families struggling with the same issues and sense of disconnectedness on a daily basis. I'm also not surprised to learn about new studies pointing to the increase in depression and behavioral problems among children who are plugged in all day, every day and consume an enormous amount of social media that takes them away from their families. According to the Kaiser Family Foundation, the average young American spends practically every waking minute—except for the time in school—using a smart phone, computer, television, or other electronic device. And when you factor in the multitasking component (i.e., surfing the web and listening to music at the same time) they can pack nearly eleven hours of media content into just seven and a half hours!

Strong links have been found between the number of hours spent "connected" and negative results like obesity, low grades, depression, behavioral problems, and social withdrawal. It may sound counterintuitive to think being a consumer of so much social media can lead to social withdrawal, but the truth is that connecting through electronics is completely different from face-to-face human interaction. It's easy to confuse being "connected" with real communication. A teenager, for example, who locks himself in a room alone, tethered to gadgets and all of their artificial, contrived forms of "connection" may find himself moving farther away from true connections and genuine communication that enrich the heart and soul.

It's becoming increasingly more challenging to deal with a child who has been exposed to modern technology at a very young age and uses it daily. And it's not just your children who are relying on technology to communicate. How many times a day do you text your child or partner or friends? How often do you come home to a house where people are locked away playing games, watching TV, or chatting online so that your entry into your own home is greeted by silence? How often do you eat in front of the TV because it's easier than having to communicate? How many hours of uninterrupted minutes do you spend with your children or partner every day? If you're game, now is the time to be the change agent in your household and provide the best life possible for your family by embracing the *Stripped Down Challenge*. The whole idea of stripping stuff out of the house that keeps you disconnected from others or from achieving the life you deserve (e.g., TV, cell phone) will start to get you back in touch with the people you love and live with.

So, does this sound like you? If you're not sure if your family could use the *Stripped Down Challenge*, answer the following questions.

1. Our kids send more than 3,000 text messages a month.   YES   NO
2. We eat dinner together as a family fewer than three times a week.   YES   NO
3. We sometimes text a family member when they are in the house.   YES   NO
4. We own more than three TVs.   YES   NO
5. Each bedroom in the house has a TV.   YES   NO
6. Each person has his or her own computer.   YES   NO
7. We have to pry the kids away from the TV to get them to school.   YES   NO
8. I have to pry my partner away from the TV to get his/her attention   YES   NO
9. We answer email or send text messages while speaking to other family members.   YES   NO
10. We eat dinner in front of the TV.   YES   NO
11. It seems like we just don't talk to each other anymore.   YES   NO
12. We watch TV more than we talk to each other.   YES   NO
13. A lot of our bonding time is spent at the mall or running between the kids' activities.   YES   NO
14. I want to get my family more connected to each other.   YES   NO

If you answered YES to seven or more of these questions, then you're a prime candidate for the *Stripped Down Challenge*!

Here's how is starts—and trust me, it's painful! Your whole family is about to go cold turkey for a week by swearing off technology and working to get to know each other again. Below are my rules for taking my seven-day *Stripped Down Challenge*. I know they're tough but if you're struggling to feel like a real "family," and you are serious about changing then I suggest you try it, and see what happens.

The Rules (to be adhered to for a total of seven days):

- *No cell phones, texting, or PDAs.* Talk to other people in person. The short texts you are used to sending and receiving may just turn into real conversations!
- *No electronics—that includes the TV, games, and the internet.* Instead, institute family game nights, nightly story time or a daily walk to the park. By the end of the week, your family will realize the greatest entertainment in life comes from spending time with one another.
- *Prepare and eat healthy meals together.* Quitting junk food and making healthy meals together is an instant way to reconnect.
- *Practice the Trash Bag Tango once a day to clean and organize the house.* Give everyone two trash bags; one is for any trash or recyclables that might be lying around the house—empty take-out food containers, old newspapers or magazines, soiled and unusable clothing. The second is for items that you no longer need, use, or want—items that you intend to sell, give away, donate to a worthy cause. Set the kitchen timer and go for it for just ten minutes! When family members (including you) come across items that they cannot let go of, challenge each other to see whether those things reflect true needs or wants. As you all add stuff to the pile of things you are getting rid of, have everyone attach a dollar amount to it. Encourage everyone to "own" what they are getting rid of so that they understand the colossal waste of time, effort, energy, and money spent on buying that thing, bringing it home, and storing it. This clutter has depleted not just your bank account, but also your personal life. For example, a teenager cleaning her room may decide that two pairs of nearly new jeans can go because they aren't in style anymore or they "just don't fit right." When an item was expensive to purchase, the decision to discard it because it will never be used is a tough one. But there's a great lesson here for everyone! This exercise will help change the way your family thinks about their possessions and how they shop in the future.

Don't feel like you have to overhaul the entire house in a single day or even a week; see what happens over these seven days. Just by giving each person in the family this simple ten-minute task to complete each day, you will definitely put a dent in the physical clutter.

- *At least once a day each family member needs to tell every other member of the family something that they like about them and say, "I love you," to that person.* This will definitely feel forced and unnatural at first but it helps everyone in the family get into the habit of saying what they love and appreciate about others.

- *For moms and dads—have a date night!* This is an important way for you as a couple to start reconnecting. Giving yourselves a night when it's just the two of you to talk, laugh, and remember why you love each other is an important way to strengthen your relationship. Take your first date night during the seven-day challenge, but you must start making it a ritual in your home. Don't skip this! One night once a month to connect and catch up (without the kids or other distractions) is worth a hundred weeks of vacation at the end of the year. And while you are out, the no TV, games, internet rule stays in place for your kids!

- And last, but definitely not least—*no recreational shopping!*

Every night at dinner check in with each other about how things are going. Believe me, everyone will have an opinion and you'll hear them loud and clear! Encourage everyone to persevere. Although it will seem endless, it's only a week and I promise the results can transform your family and your life.

At the end of the week, plan a big family meeting and sit together to talk about the experience of being "stripped down." What worked? What didn't? Ask each member of the family the following:

- What was the hardest rule to follow during the past seven days?
- What was the easiest rule to follow during the past seven days?
- What did you like best about the experience?

- What did you like least?
- What can you permanently change based on your experience? For example, can you limit your "plugged in" hours (web surfing, texting, watching television, etc.) to certain hours of the day?
- How did this experience make you feel? Did your feelings change throughout the week?
- Did you learn anything about yourself or your family that you didn't know?
- If you had to live by just one rule, what would that be?
- If you could add a rule to live by, which may or may not be among the above rules, what would that be?

It's important, however, for the Challenge not to end here. Take the positive things from the experience, talk about what worked and what didn't. The rules for the first week of the Challenge are deliberately extreme and need modifying if they are going to fit into a daily routine for you and your family. Communicate and negotiate with everyone in your home to rewrite the rules in a way that works for your whole family. For example, you could create a no phones or cell phones period during meals (this includes breakfast and it includes you). You might cut back the amount of time everyone spends in front of the TV. You could create a meal schedule that includes the kids being responsible for preparing one meal a week.

FIVE NEW RULES

Make a list of your family's five rules after you've completed the Stripped Down Challenge:

1. _____

2. _____

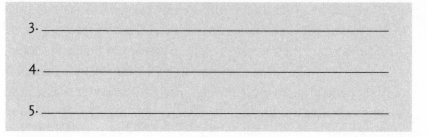

3. _____

4. _____

5. _____

If there were one element of the Challenge I'd encourage you to continue, that would be the regular family dinners together with no TV and no disruptions. Make Saturday mornings the time every person picks up the clutter they've let build up during the week, or institute a regular family meeting to talk about issues—including money and finances—that affect everyone in the home. Whatever rules you decide on, make sure they're agreed to by all and are in the best interest of every person in your home. If everyone agrees to the ongoing rules, there's a higher chance of people committing to them.

KEEP THE FUTURE IN PLAIN VIEW

Clarity is key to success. Never lose sight of your vision or your future. No matter the type of clutter—physical, emotional, or financial—if you find yourself stuck when deciding which items go and which should stay, always go back to that vision of where you want to be and how you really want to live. It's human nature to fall back on our emotions, excuses, and to let our memories and desires (and exhaustion) get the best of us. But we do have a choice. We always have a choice. It's like driving a car. You *can* go 100 miles per hour if you want, and you *can* drive over a cliff if you want, and you *can* go down a dangerous road rather than taking the safer route. But those wouldn't be wise decisions to make, and you wouldn't dare do any such thing with your kids in the car. You strive to protect them and their future every single day, so why not look at your life the same way?

Clearing out the clutter in your home—physical, emotional, or financial—won't be a one-time (or one-week) event. From now on you'll be talking yourself through each and every purchase, and hopefully you can instill the same decision-making process in every family member. Remember to ask yourself, does this thing fulfill a specific purpose that moves me closer to my (and my family's) vision? Will it be as important to me next year as I think it will be today? Is my "need" to have this thing really just an excuse to make me feel better? Am I letting my emotions dictate this purchase? Does this thing satisfy a true need or a disguised want? You need to be having these conversations with your kids, too, as they come to you asking for money or for you to buy them something. Eventually they learn to have the conversation with themselves before coming to see you.

As I mentioned earlier, unless you've trained your children from a very early age to appreciate the value of money, space, and possessions in a manner that minimizes clutter and nonessentials, then there will be an inevitable breaking-in period for them. If you've given them all they ever wanted—and more—since birth, and the word "No" is foreign to them, then chances are this will be a period of immense growing pains and strife. They may not want to touch anything in their rooms or see anything happen to the other rooms of the house. They may continue to expect anything and everything from you, scoffing at the thought of sticking to a budget. They may call you all sorts of names and hold steadfastly to their bloated expectations and unrealistic sense of money. And they may resist you in a way you've never seen before, especially if this is the first time you're taking a stand and owning up to your family's financial problems.

Keep coming back to the vision that the whole family has for your home, your finances, and your shared life together. Remember that you are doing this for the benefit and the welfare of the whole family, and to ensure you can provide for everyone's future needs.

Everyone can certainly have a say about which items go and which can stay. For every one item someone refuses to touch, encourage him or her to relinquish another item. As your children mature and get used to this new way of living, they will begin to appreciate more why you've made these choices today, and behaving attuned to the goals you're setting now will become second nature. They'll eventually find it easier to let go of items that have lost their value and importance, and they'll have a newfound sense of needs versus wants that they will carry with them wherever they go. What you're doing today with the tools you're practicing in this book may be one of the most important lessons you'll give your children as they mature into thoughtful, productive (and clutter-free!) adults.

REALITY CHECK BEFORE YOU CHECK OUT

Be mindful. Ask yourself the following questions before you make any purchase:

Will this item move me closer or farther away from the vision I have for the life I want?

Is this a want or a need?

Will I value this item next year as much as I do today?

Can I afford it? Can my family afford it?

What will I not buy in order to buy this item?

What will this item replace?

What will I get rid of to make space for this item?

What do I expect this item to do for me today, tomorrow, and in the future?

Pause Before Purchase!

Dear Peter:

I wanted you to know that my husband and I have done well since we saw you on *Oprah* and committed to cleaning up. We resist bringing more stuff into the house, especially now that our three kids are grown and gone. Plus, when the "stuff" got tossed, our minds cleared enough to focus on eliminating the debt that had accumulated as we finished putting our kids through college and paid for our daughter's wedding. In about nine months, ending *before* the economy tanked, we got rid of $68,000 in debt (representing nearly half of our annual income), plus built up a significant emergency fund. With all we've now lost in the stock market, we rest much easier knowing that our only debt is our mortgage, and that we have more than a two-thirds equity in our house. *Amazing* how one good discipline leads to the next! Get rid of the junk and then tackle the finances! My rear end, however, still looks too big. I'm ready to tackle it next . . .

PERSONAL ACTION PLAN FOR YOUR HOME

Get clarity: Take an objective look at your stuff and do not let emotions or endless excuses get in the way of making changes. Stay true to your vision when you take inventory of your belongings and it will be easier to deal with letting certain items go. Your home is a reflection of you, and what is in your home is a reflection of your financial state. If your home is peaceful, together, organized, clean, clutter-free, and purposeful, then other areas of your life, such as your finances, emotions, relationships, and sense of well-being will reflect that.

Get real: You can't do this alone. You need to include your loved ones in the conversation and action plan for cleaning up your home (and life!). Create a collective vision as a family unit that is in addition to your individual visions. Be mindful and respectful of each other. Make room for patience and compromise just as you're making room for what's really important for you and yours.

Get going: Plan your first family meeting. If you need to, plan your first meeting with your partner and then, as a team, alert your family about the time and place where you'll all get together and go over the family's finances and what everyone needs to do to participate. If opening up to your partner about money is terrifying, use the script I outlined on page 94 to help get you started. This is not a conversation you want to place in the "can wait" pile. If you can only commit to doing just one thing in a week, then choose the exact time and place when you approach your honey about money and start talking! And if you need just one (less stressful) thing to do today . . .

A task for today: Make a commitment to spend just ten minutes every day this week collecting things in your home that you no longer need, use, or want. As you are doing so, think about when and where you'll have the family meeting, or just that first one with your partner. Map it all out in your head so you're prepared. Be strong. Be proactive. Make it happen!

part three

From Today to Tomorrow
and Beyond

9

Checkup and Maintenance

WE ROUTINELY CHECK IN on so many things in our lives to maintain them properly. We keep an eye on the gas gauge in our car. We spot repairs to make at home. We hop on the scale once in a while to check our weight and visit the doctors once a year to check our heart and lungs. We ask if something is wrong with loved ones when they appear to be hurting or frustrated. And we frequently run checkups throughout the day on ourselves when we glance in the mirror to address our hair, clothes, makeup, or to avoid that piece of parsley stuck in our front teeth after a meal. In fact, our list of things to maintain in life is seemingly endless. But why do we avoid maintaining that same level of awareness and attention to our possessions, homes, finances, and even what's bothering us psychologically?

You know why by now. All that stuff—all that debt and clutter—holds our emotional baggage, too. We can't separate out the emotions, so they get stuck and they stay stuck in our stuff and debt until they get to a point that we just simply stop, look around, and decide to finally deal with it all. As I've said, it does you no good to clean up once and think you're "done." Attacking the problem like a one-hit wonder won't do you any good. You've missed the point of this whole book if you go through your audits, change the way you deal with what you own and what you owe, but then shove this book on a shelf to collect dust until you pull it out a year or two later to repeat the same exercises.

You must make a commitment to maintaining this part of your life forever as you would your health or car. This will require daily, monthly, and annual checkups. Your washing machine (yep—you heard me right!) has a great lesson to teach us here. Think for a second of what happens if you put a load of soiled clothing into your washing machine, let it run for five minutes or so and then turn it off and come back a week later. We both know what you have—a stinky, mildewed, smelly mess. If you don't let the machine finish the cycle this is what you'll end up with every time. Your life is not that different. If you don't "finish the cycle" of things that you do every day, then you're sure to end up with a stinking mess of one kind or another. If you open something, close it. If you start an important conversation with your partner, finish it. If you use something up, replenish it. If you dirty something, clean it. If you think about engaging your children in a list of tasks to complete, speak up and invite them. If you break something, repair it. This is what completing the cycle is all about. If you open the mail and throw it onto the kitchen counter, you're not completing the cycle. If you want to address the tension in your life by getting your kids to spend less money at the mall on the weekend and spend more time hanging out with the family at home, schedule a family meeting and start a dialogue with them—or you won't be completing the cycle. If you don't pay bills at the end of the month, you're not completing the cycle. It's that simple. We're not that different from our washing machines!

Everything in life has a cycle. The sun rises and sets. We are active during the day and we sleep at night. The seasons and calendar years reflect cycles. In human terms, we are born one day and will die on another day. In between that larger cycle, we cycle through billions of other kinds of smaller cycles to stay alive and alert, as well as productive, thoughtful, and loving beings. Our day-to-day patterns should cycle all the way through; we need to complete all those little cycles that make up the larger, and much more profound cycle that is our life.

> Dear Peter:
> I have found some amazing gifts from being made redundant; the most precious was spending profoundly delightful time with my ailing mother, and being able to write her family history and then create two books for her.
> Previously I was an overworked stressed workaholic and it is so liberating not to have all that went with it! Also my health has started to improve, I am decluttering as I go, relearning the art of baking, losing weight, laughing much more and caring much less about people's opinion of me . . . or is that just old age?

If you've succeeded in going through the audits, the house, the bills, and your emotions, and you've balanced those out against your vision, then now it's time to learn the ropes of keeping it all in check—of completing the cycle. In this final chapter, I'll give you my rules for the new road you're on. Don't panic if you're reading this chapter and you feel a bit unprepared to dive into this material because you're still getting over (or perhaps going through) your audits. I encourage you to read this chapter more than once. Come back to it as a guide for keeping your home in order.

RESPECT THE LAW OF CHAOS

Let me start by stating a simple fact: the universal law of chaos is real. It is the reason it's impossible for a clean room to stay that way without further intervention. I won't bore you with the technical, scientific details of the laws of thermodynamics, but simply stated, the second law of thermodynamics states that things go from a state of order to disorder. In other words, systems will break down unless they have some input of energy. In less scientific terms, you need to get off your butt and make an effort to maintain what you have if you want to keep it clean, uncluttered, and organized!

Of course this applies to maintaining our homes, our personal happiness, and keeping our finances in order. When you let the tensions in your life go unaddressed, they quickly fester and gnaw at the root of your soul and sense of well-being. When you let debt run free, it rapidly becomes disordered and chaotic. When you let your home become overrun with stuff, disorder sets in every facet of your life, not just your physical space, as we've seen. The solution is to direct your energy back into these systems—your self, your home, and your life—to bring them back to order. And it's not that hard to do when you do it consistently. The amount of energy you'll need to put into maintaining your entire self on a routine basis will pale in comparison to the amount of energy it takes to do a complete overhaul once you've let chaos have its way again. Think about it this way: Is it easier to put energy into losing ten pounds or one hundred pounds? Is it easier to get rid of $1,000 of debt or $10,000? How about clearing up a cluttered counter top versus an entire room?

I'm probably sounding like a broken record by now. Let's get to those details.

VISION REVISION

After you feel like you've done your best with the exercises in this book, you should be on the road to achieving your ideal vision. But that vision will still need finessing along the way; not even a vision can remain stuck in time. It evolves and grows as you do. It must be revisited often as circumstances in your life change and situations emerge that have an effect on your vision, or that of your family's.

One of my mantras is to live in the present. This doesn't mean that you don't plan for your future and regard that future in your current decisions. Keep your vision present and up to date. This will make all of your maintenance tasks easier and you'll have a clearer idea what, exactly, to do to maintain the order in your life.

Before you tackle any room, bill, or source of tension in your life, always come back to that all-important vision. Hold it squarely at the back of your mind and use it to motivate and inspire your decluttering actions.

DON'T EQUATE VALUE WITH COST

I've said it a million times and I'll say it again and again. Do the math of cost and value. Cost is what you're willing to pay. Value is what it's truly worth. Let's take an example that has nothing to do with clutter. Picture a used car. It has a sticker price of $8,000 but it has a sketchy transmission. How much is it really worth to you? Would you pay that $8,000 only to learn next week that you have to put $2,000 into it to fix the tranny? Maybe it's worth only $6,000? Value and cost don't mean the same thing. If it did, then Wall Street wouldn't operate the way it does today. When a stock sells for $40 a share, is that what it's really worth? Or is that price just a reflection of what investors are willing to pay for it right now? When it shoots up to $50 a share tomorrow, or drops to $35, what's its true value?

When it comes to your physical and mental space, your time, and your energy, you have to separate out the real value of these things to you and the cost you bear when you don't delineate cost from value. How much is that debt really costing you not just in dollar signs but also in emotional stability and stress? What's the price of a bad relationship that impedes the path to your vision? What's the opportunity cost of lost time spent rummaging for lost keys or a piece of paper with an important note written on it? Wouldn't you rather spend lost minutes decluttering than running around in frantic frustration?

I'll say this again, too: no matter whether you own or rent your space, you're paying per square foot. Space has value, too. If the stuff in your space is driving you nuts, then step up and do something about it. It won't fix itself on its own. Giving time to what you value is important. When you lose your ability to enjoy a room or to store your car and seasonable items in a tidy garage, you're throwing that portion of your rent or mortgage down the drain. When you rent storage space you're throwing good money after bad space rather than solving the problem. By relying on "later" to deal with things you're really bowing to the power of your stuff to control you. Wrestling back that power, making a decision, dealing with the stuff are all concrete ways of moving your life forward and making choices for a better you.

As soon as you calculate the real cost of clutter you'll realize that it's not worth holding onto things because of their value—because of what they're seemingly worth. And when you calculate the total cost of your debt, you don't even have to look at the dollar signs to realize your debt is immeasurable.

FIVE MINUTES HERE, TEN MINUTES THERE

Remember, ten to fifteen short minutes can transform a life. Really. You'd be amazed at how much you can accomplish in that time period. Every day, take five minutes to stop and think about how you're feeling and whether there's a pressure point somewhere deep within you that should be addressed before it surfaces. Take another five or ten minutes to straighten up an untidy small area in your home or mill through your bills and organize them in your home office system. Those small projects and attention to details really add up.

Make it a goal to go through these daily exercises at the same time. You may, for example, choose to do a five-minute meditation first thing in the morning and then perform a quick, five-minute cleanup before the kids get up; sort the mail and bills after they go to bed. Make them daily rituals like eating breakfast or taking a multivitamin.

Dear Peter:

I worked for (the same company) for twenty-two years until I was laid off last year. Fortunately for me, I was eligible for early retirement. I have been waiting for this opportunity for at least ten years but felt that I had to tough it out so I could qualify for retirement after so many years with the company (literally, a lifetime!). Now, at age forty-five with a year's severance, I have the opportunity to look at new options. Truth be told, it has given me the opportunity to clear the clutter in my life—I was living proof that your clutter is a reflection of other stuff that is not right in your life. I have spent quite a bit of time cleaning out my house, donating to charity, and organizing all over the place! My whole demeanor has changed and I love my life, and I could not say that last year.

MONTHLY MAINTENANCE

Though you'll be doing your daily and weekly purges, cleanups, and bill paying, it helps to have monthly focal points that reflect the particular time of year. For example, during November and December, the holidays take over our lives and bring with them their own set of challenges, and, you guessed it, clutter. For this reason, I've created a month-by-month calendar that you can use to keep all of that in check, too.

The Calendar for an Organized Life

January	February	March
Renewal	Paper Play	Tension Tamer
April	*May*	*June*
Dollars & Sense	In Memoriam	Summer Summit
July	*August*	*September*
Americana	Back-to-School	Season Opener
October	*November*	*December*
Winter Warm-Up	'Tis the Season	Celebrate

January: Renewal

Take a deep, cleansing breath. I won't ask you about New Year's resolutions or to commit to losing twenty pounds (finally!) this year. Did you know that the first Monday after New Year's is the busiest day of the year for both divorce lawyers and travel agents? And that one million boxes of smoking cessation gum, lozenges, and patches are sold in January? Yes, January is a month of new beginnings and fresh starts but its implied demands often set us up for failure. Come January 1, millions of us resolve to eat better, get new jobs, and ditch their vices—and guess what: businesses make millions from that newfound resolve. From quitting smoking to diet books to gym sign-ups, the amount of money (despite a newfound resolve to deal with debt) we spend to better ourselves is colossal. Good money gets thrown to good intentions, but bad results. According to some statistics, 25 percent of people who make New Year's resolutions fail after just one week.

So here's my advice for you this month. Pick a single, doable thing you can do differently that will move you closer to your vision. Just one. Don't set yourself up for failure by committing to unrealistic expectations. If you do that one, itty-bitty thing well, it will inspire you to do more, and more the next month. Maybe your one thing will be to take just one piece of advice in this book and execute it, such as spending five minutes a day writing in a journal to focus on just you—your thoughts and emotions. Or perhaps your one thing will be to make a homemade meal once a week instead of ordering out or picking up prepared food. Or your one thing could be scheduling the time to speak candidly with your significant other about what you've learned in this book and what you plan to do with the information.

Just one thing. It can relate to any part of your vision. Let your entire renewal process commence with that one single thing. As I've been saying, giant leaps happen over the course of several little steps. Take a single step this month and watch what happens.

February: Paper Play

Taxes may not be due for another several weeks, but it's not fun dealing with those at the last minute. Prepare your taxes and file this month if you can to ensure a quick refund (or be done thinking about writing a check to the IRS). Discard and shred financial records and other documentation that you no longer need to back up your returns (see box on page 256 for your paperwork cheat sheet). You'll find that papers that seemed important six months ago are irrelevant now. I'm convinced that 80 percent of what goes into a filing cabinet never sees the light of day again. Perhaps a few months of unnecessary utility bills have crept into your files. It's incredibly difficult to throw away files. After all, at some point in time you thought this piece of paper was so valuable that it deserved to be filed. And now you're going to just . . . throw it away? The answer is, yes. Label and file current tax records.

I dealt a lot with paperwork and filing in *It's All Too Much: An Easy Plan for Living a Richer Life with Less Stuff* and I encourage you to refer to that book for the finer details of managing your financial records for tax season. Check with your own accountant or financial adviser to verify that this information is up to date and accurate for your state and situation.

PAPERWORK CHEAT SHEET

Come on, fess up: when you went digging into your financial clutter, you found some ancient receipts that you can no longer read, and tax returns dating back before your children were born. What should be kept and what can be tossed? Here's my cheat sheet for keeping all that paperwork at bay.

Every month:
- Toss out ATM, bank deposit slips, and credit card receipts after you have checked them against your bank or credit card statements.
- Toss out receipts for minor purchases—unless there is a warranty or refund involved.

Every year:
- Toss out your monthly bank and credit card statements (unless you require proof of deductions for taxation purposes)—most credit card companies provide a year-end summary that you can retain.
- Toss out monthly mortgage statements, provided you receive a year-end summary of your account.
- Toss out pay stubs after they are checked against your W-2 or 1099.
- Toss out your W-2 and 1099 forms from seven years ago and earlier.

- Toss out canceled checks and receipts or annual statements for:
  - mortgage interest from seven years ago and earlier
  - property taxes from seven years ago and earlier
  - deductible business expenses or other tax-deductible expenses from seven years ago and earlier

Keep indefinitely:
- Annual tax returns.
- Year-end summary statements from financial institutions.
- Receipts for the purchase of any investments you own.
- Receipts for home improvement costs or major purchases that may be needed for insurance claims or similar.

If you want to check the official word on this, read what Uncle Sam has to say at the website of the Internal Revenue Service. Download Publication No. 552 at IRS.gov for complete details of what to keep and what you can let go of to keep the tax man happy.

March: Tension Tamer

Gotcha. Just when you thought I was going to have you do the traditional spring-clean job, I'm surprising you with this, similar to the "just one" approach in January. I want you to pick one area in your life—just one, but try to choose the one that you think deserves the greatest amount of your attention and energy—and focus on the vision of that one area this month. My hope is that you pick the one area of your life that is causing you the most tension, and that you address it head-on. This is the month when, for the majority of people living in the United States, the clocks move forward an hour into daylight saving time. You may lose an hour of sleep that second Sunday of the month, but look at it as an opportunity to "spring forward" and move past a troubling area in your life that propagates pain and struggle. Don't put another Band-Aid on it through shopping or avoiding. Like I said before, face your fear and ditch denial. Have the difficult conversation with yourself or with another person involved. Make it a goal to reach April 1st with a lighter load.

When I helped Susan go through this exercise with me, she picked a habit of avoiding the gym on the weekend to go shopping as her focal point. After probing a bit further, it was evident that she wasn't happy about her weight and that her struggles to shed twenty pounds had pushed her farther into the zone where she hated exercise and avoided it at all costs now. She filled that hole with routine shopping excursions, one of which took place every Saturday morning when her husband went to the gym. I asked her if she would get any joy in going with him, or in taking a group exercise class with a friend on Saturdays. After a long pause, she admitted that it would be enjoyable, and that part of her reason for avoiding any form of exercise was because she hated the "alone" factor. She saw shopping as her friend, and exercise as her enemy where she was stuck in a solitary place of misery both physically and emotionally.

As soon as Susan began to see the pleasure she could experience in exercise with people she loved, she decided to make plans every Saturday morning to have an exercise companion. She realized, too, that she didn't necessarily have to go to the gym or do a formal class. She could schedule a hike in the nearby hills with a neighbor, go for a bike ride with a friend, or even speed-walk the mall when the weather was too cold or rainy to be outside.

Again, I challenge you to ask yourself where the tension is in your life. How do you try to avoid it or "shop" around it? Use the month of March to take more time exploring your sources of tension and do what you can to tame them. March is typically the month we begin to look toward warmer weather and the onset of spring. Rather than burden yourself with the thought of traditional spring cleaning, just choose one area of your mind to spring clean. It will surely lead to all other forms of "cleaning."

April: Dollars & Sense

Taxes are out of the way this month. You either got some money in return or you owed the IRS. Your new fiscal year has begun. Use this month to double-check on bills and balances. How are you doing in your debt clean-up? Are you watching your monthly balances go down? Did you have an unexpected expense last year that inspired you to plan better for this next tax year? Have you been socking away money for an emergency fund if you currently don't have one that will last you at least six months of living expenses? How is your family's "vision fund" coming along? Review your budget and schedule an appointment with your financial advisor if you have one. If you got a big check back from the IRS, you may want to review your income withholdings so you keep more of that money in your pocket during the year to help pay down your debt and allocate to savings each month. Be careful what you do with your tax refund. Make it work for your vision; don't fritter it away.

Now is also a good time to update any insurance policies or legal documents such as wills as appropriate. Make photocopies of any new policies, credit cards, or other critical documents acquired in the last twelve months and store the copies away from your home in a secure location.

May: In Memoriam

Memorial Day isn't until the end of the month, but see if you can use this month to clear out the clutter you have the hardest time dealing with: the clutter that conceals your deepest, sometimes darkest and gut-wrenching memories. The box of old children's clothes in your basement or attic. Remnants of your parents' and grandparents' lives lying in your attic—their heirlooms, the old furniture you inherited, piles of decaying paperwork and paraphernalia you never knew what to do with before, the boxes of cobwebbed and yellowed photos, and god-knows-what. Save your love letters, but throw away the emblems of your past that are long over and that no longer serve a definite, vision-forwarding purpose in your life today. Let go of the things that take up space and dust and preserve only that which is worthy of displaying in loving memory of people who once represented those objects. Do justice to your memories. Honor them appropriately.

June: Summer Summit

Hard to believe, but June is about the middle of the calendar year. How are you doing? What is your family up to this summer? Now that the kids are out of school, their obligations and commitments have changed. They may not have to worry so much about essays, tests, and homework as they move into other activities to fill the gap between the new and the old school year. Their daily routines will shift depending on what they are doing over the summer months, and they will likely have extra time to devote to whatever it is you want them to. Suffice it to say the summer affords you a great opportunity to capitalize on their extra time and bring everyone together as a family to focus on establishing or reaffirming the family vision.

Think of it as a more comprehensive family meeting. You can take inventory as a family of what you have and have not achieved yet this year. Rather than wait for the new school year, which is sure to be hectic and crazy-busy in the very beginning, set some goals now that your children can begin to work toward so when the first day of school arrives, they are already in gear. You may, for example, want to revisit the household chores—who does what and when— and resolve any tension or conflict in this regard now. Create a job chart that will be adhered to until further notice. Have everyone keep track of which chores they accomplish in a single week and the time they spent on each one. At your next family meeting, share the charts and adjust as necessary. Make each member of the family responsible for keeping his or her personal space and belongings clean and clutter free. To make things fair, you may want to rotate certain household chores on a weekly or biweekly basis so the same person isn't stuck always washing the dishes or walking the dog and cleaning out the kitty litter box.

To help keep all the chores and accomplishments in check, designate a specific area in your home to post the job chart. This can also be a place where your family calendar is displayed and where you can post important announcements, phone numbers, emergency contacts, reminders, messages, mail addressed to everyone, and invitations. You can hang your keys and keep your loose change in this area. Just make sure this spot doesn't become overrun with stuff, too. On Sunday night, or the day of your choice, go through this message center and clear out the old to make way for the new in the coming week.

July: Americana

The Fourth of July reminds us of our national pastimes, so what better month to celebrate the sport of selling our used goods on the front lawn. Yes, I'm talking about the old-fashioned yard sale. A yard sale can be a useful—and profitable—way to help keep the clutter from creeping back into your home. If you don't want to do it all on your own, then bring your community together and enlist a few neighbors to join in with you. Trust me, you won't be the only one who needs to unload some stuff. The more, the merrier—stuff and yard-sale participants. Some tips to a successful sale:

Set a date. Do this well in advance, not the night before. Skip the Fourth if it lands on a weekend.

Decide what to sell as a family. In addition to the things you've collected from purging, give everyone in your family a box or two that they can fill with additional items they are ready to sell.

Find a pattern among the goods for sale and sort accordingly. Organize the items for sale and box similar items. This will save time later when you are setting up. Store everything neatly in the garage.

Spread the word. Advertise. Post large, colorful signs on a major road with directions and a map. Try listing the yard sale online or in free community papers. Word-of-mouth can be the most powerful, though, so tell your neighbors and your friends. Send an email around and mention it on your Facebook page. If anyone asks to add their own set of goods, by all means, let them! The more sellers, the more buyers you can attract.

Attach price tags but be ready to bargain. Clearly price everything with masking tape and bright markers. Use tables to make the viewing of merchandise easier. Borrow clothing racks, and have a great layout of goods so people can easily see everything. Don't get stingy. The idea of a yard sale is to get rid of everything. Don't walk away from a haggler! Let people bargain. Offer to add items for an extra 50 cents or offer five books for the price of three. An hour before closing, slash prices.

Enlist helpers. Assign your helpers specific tasks like managing the crowds, answering questions, making sales, taking payments, and providing laughter and fun. Designate one person to manage the money. Have a lot of small change handy; whoever deals with the money should wear a fanny pack to keep it safe and in one place.

Be prepared. Have an extension cord handy so people can check electric items. Have shopping bags or boxes handy to help people collect and carry goods away.

Aim to get rid of everything. Whatever doesn't sell does *not* go back into your garage or basement. Drop it right into your charity bag or arrange for a charity to pick it up.

August: Back-to-School

The new school year is upon you and your kids. New teachers. New syllabuses. New schedules. New stresses. New routines. New chaos. New sources of anxiety, clutter, and debt.

Life might have slowed down a bit during June and July, but the start of school ushers in a new pace. The family car will metaphorically go from zero to sixty overnight when that first day of school arrives. If you're not already in gear to go at this pace, the reentry can be excruciating. In addition to your family's main budget, it helps to create a mini-budget for dealing with your school-related items like new clothes and gear, and home office and school supplies. Try to avoid buying enough school supplies to equip an entire classroom. See what is still useful from the previous year so you don't make duplicate or unnecessary purchases. Check your home office, too. Your children don't need their own fancy set of scissors when yours will do just fine.

Be especially careful about digital gadgets in the new school year. Your kids will be comparing their electronics with their friends that first day of school. Will your son have the latest smart phone? Does your daughter's laptop computer beat out her classmate's outdated model? Get real about what you want your children to value in this department. They don't need the latest and greatest gadget to succeed in their academic life—no matter what they tell you or how hard they cry. Invite your children to write up a list of what they think they need for the new school year and have them prioritize that list. Check it against what they already have. The summer months may have, in fact, affected their expectations if they spent it playing video games and playing with their friends at the mall. Make the back-to-school month a back-to-basics month. And don't forget to keep up with your family meetings. Think about how they will best work out in the changing schedule of the calendar school year. Try to plan for your upcoming family meetings now so they don't get canceled at the last minute due to school-related conflicts.

September: Season Opener

Fall is fast approaching. The stores have already started to stock Halloween decorations, tempting you to shop, and you can't wear your shorts and T-shirts any longer now that the weather has started to shift. Use this month to go through your wardrobe and switch out the summer clothes for the fall and winter clothes. As you do this sorting, you'll find plenty to pull out of your wardrobe forever. Don't think twice about an article of clothing you never wore during the summer, or that skipped the last winter entirely. Get rid of it.

October: Winter Warm-Up

If you live in a climate where winters tend to be long and cold, then come October, winter is already on your mind because the shorter days and nippier nighttime temperatures are cluing you in to its approach. Make a list of the chores you need to complete to winterize your home. Divvy up those chores appropriately among family members. Raking and picking up leaves. Cleaning out the gutters on your home. Installing storm windows and putting winter tires on your car. Putting away the gardening tools and, if you try to squeeze your car into the garage during the winter months, reorganizing the garage to make it fit. Reorganize? Correction: *declutter* the garage. Use this month to put your cleaning efforts on the garage.

Dear Peter:
After I pledged to clean my messy house, I began with two garbage bags, ten minutes a day. If I missed a day, I would do twenty minutes the next. When I stopped tracking time, it didn't matter! You had already started the process in my head that it was okay to do the elephant approach with one bite at a time, and the stress was gone! Before the holidays I just kept

going and before I knew it I was finished! I had done "Spring Cleaning" in December! Cleaned from scratch, removed clutter, got organized—all before Christmas and the New Year. Now my resolution is to maintain the organization and keep the process going. And because I am organized I can now concentrate on more important goals.

The most wonderful thing of all is during the entire process items began appearing that were in their original wrapping with tags on. I wrapped them as presents. A scarf set, a purse, jewelry, etc. On Christmas Eve I took the items along with two bags of gently worn clothing and drove to a dark neighborhood. On the corner was a little modest house with a string of Christmas lights on the porch. I knocked on the door and no one came, then all of a sudden a woman drove up into the driveway. A wonderful experience beyond words occurred. It left me with tears of gratefulness and joy.

No longer will I look at a mammoth project and just freeze and do nothing because it just looks like too much!

November: 'Tis the Season

Halloween barely ended and the stores are already rife with Christmas clutter. The retailers are working hard to get your attention, and your dollars. At the back of your mind sit your good intentions but in the front of your mind and before your eyes sits a world of temptation. Pre-Christmas sales. Buy now, pay later offers (zero down and no interest until 2015!). Gift-giving pressures. Buffet tables at office parties and holiday mixers. Where will you draw the line? How will you white-knuckle your way through the next two months?

You won't have to white-knuckle your way through any of it. Just plan and prepare with your vision, as always, at the real forefront of your mind. Plan everything, from your gift giving to how you want to spend the day after Thanksgiving (not at the mall!) and your New

Year's Eve. Don't give in to societal pressures to spend, spend, spend this season and give of yourself to everyone and everything. Keep your big goals and dreams in check at all times. The holidays can bring lots of tension and stress, so be sure to check in with yourself and go back to your personal audit whenever you feel the need. The busyness of the season also makes for a lack of communication among family members. When's the last time you asked your partner how he or she is doing? How are your kids handling what's stressing them out at school and home?

December: Celebrate!

You made it through another year. I'm a huge fan of celebrating successes. Big and small. Take time this month to enjoy the season, your family, the goals you've met this year, and the steps you've taken toward your achievements. Take comfort in the fact you're setting a foundation for your future peace of mind, the security of your loved ones, and the realization of that vision. If you've diligently been working through the year doing your best with your cleanup, checkups, and maintenance tasks, then you can bask in some of that glory this month. Take pride in how far you've come and leave room for improvement next year.

ALWAYS RENEW YOUR PATH WITH A COMMITMENT TO PERSONAL RESPONSIBILITY

As some of you might already know, I was born and raised in Australia, but America has been my home now for more than sixteen years. I love it here and am now proud to count myself as an American citizen. That said, there is no denying that culturally this country is very different from the one I was raised in. Australia and America were founded at similar times and yet they could not, in my opinion, be more different. It's some of these differences that really fascinate me.

Before I end this book and you're off on your own, I'd like to share with you one more perspective that may inspire you to make the commitment you need to make today. The concept of "rights" is something that is very much at the forefront of the American mindset. Ask any citizen and she'll quickly tell you of her rights guaranteed under the Constitution. The right to free speech, the right to bear arms, the right to privacy, and the right to vote, among others. These are fundamental to our way of life and I remember the day I became a citizen that I swore an oath to uphold them and the Constitution. However, as a new American I always felt there was something curiously absent here—there was never any discussion of the responsibilities that correspond with these rights. In the rush to claim our rights are we failing ourselves in not embracing our responsibilities? This dilemma for me is more relevant than ever in the wake of the current economic crisis.

Americans have always had a deep-rooted belief that each person can create his or her own success. We love being independent— the rights of the individual are very much enmeshed in our culture. Independence Day is one of our finest national holidays and a cornerstone of the American psyche. But somehow, that mentality of personal independence gets lost once we hit the money topic. When money gets tight or the economy turns sour, we like to point a finger elsewhere rather than hold a mirror up. We forget that our Founding Fathers tried everything in their power to ensure that Americans would thrive in independence, and I would think this entails a great deal of personal integrity, fortitude, and *responsibility*.

I've been drilling the importance of personal responsibility into your head since the beginning of this book, and I want it to be firmly planted in your mind as you move forward now and take the action you need to take control of your life. Every January first, if you want just one New Year's Resolution that's actually doable, incredibly powerful, and sustainable for the entire year, make it your goal to take full responsibility for your life every single day no matter what life throws you. And when you stumble, fall, or get into another mess, just tell yourself that it's your responsibility to get yourself out. And you will.

Remember, change starts at home. We cannot expect (nor should we ever) that our government will bail us out and fix the problems that were a collective force in the making to begin with. If there's one thing that I want you to take away from this book, it's that you can make a tremendous difference in your own life—and even in the world at large—if you commit to just cleaning up your own little space. The collective force got us all into this mess, and the collective force of every individual will get us out. Responsibility starts at home.

Once you take ownership of your life and where you are, then you can start to change and fix it. With responsibility comes a sense of reality, and sense of hope for the future. You can't have it all, but you can have a lot more happiness and stability than you've probably got now if you simply commit to taking no less than 100 percent responsibility for your life from this day forward.

New Beginnings

WE ARE LUCKY TO BE LIVING during an exciting time in the advancement of the human race. We have more access to resources and information than ever before, and can now satisfy a tremendous amount of survival needs from the comforts of home thanks to technology, computers, and the digital magic that is the internet. But all the progress and improvement that make life easier come with a hidden cost, as they can make us lazy, negligent, and, in a word, sloppy. It's ironic, for example, that we have more knowledge about health and medicine today yet we continue to suffer from serious diseases that are largely preventable through simple lifestyle changes.

By 2019, the National Institutes of Health predicts that 43 percent of Americans will be obese (not just overweight), and health expenses related to that fact will move from 9 percent to a breathtaking 21 percent of our nation's health bill. When it comes to forecasting our national debt, the numbers can be so staggering as to sound insignificant and meaningless to us. Some experts believe that by 2017–2020, the national debt will more than double and reach $28 to $30 trillion. To put this into a more manageable perspective, this amounts to a repayment of approximately $30 million per day for the next three thousand years! As of March 2009, U.S. revolving consumer debt, made up almost entirely of credit card debt, was about $950 billion. Nearly 15 percent of our disposable income is going to service this debt, and many families have debt that exceeds 40 or 50 percent of their total income. The numbers are even worse for our youngest generations. The average credit card indebted young adult household now spends nearly 24 percent of its income on debt payments, four percentage points more, on average, than young adults did in 1992.

What I find particularly odd is that we think talking about debt is more taboo than talking about politics, religion, and even our weight.

No wonder we've got problems! Our priorities are vastly misaligned. Nearly half of us are unhappy at work and shouldering massive personal and collective debt; families are under pressure and we are fearful to talk openly about it. How can we be so scared to broach a subject as straightforward and objective as money but have no qualms about throwing our ideas out about a topic as personal and subjective as religion?

With every passing year, and with ever more passing phases of new developments in our culture and society, I find that people increasingly struggle to stay afloat. I mean this on many levels—financial, physical, spiritual, and emotional. The complaint I hear the most is simply *My life is out of control!* and the state of homes and finances is a direct reflection of this chaos. Indeed, we are inundated with information, but drowning in confusing and contradictory messages. We are bombarded by technology's benefits but seduced by its endless permission slips to slack off in properly maintaining our lives. And we are eager to seek solutions to our myriad problems but unmotivated to stay on track, especially when we take the all-or-nothing approach and end up failing ourselves over and over again, whether it's with a new diet, a new resolution, or just a new way of thinking that is supposed to reprogram our way of life.

And I haven't even mentioned the happiness factor. Saying that your life is out of control as akin to saying that you're miserable. In fact, on the happiness scale worldwide, Americans don't even make the top twenty. We come in at twenty-third; Denmark claims to have the happiest people on the planet. Do the Danes live more simply? With less? I'd say so! There's so much happiness to be had in living simply within or even below your means. And we all know by now, there's so much misery lying on the road of extravagance and living beyond your means. By 2020, depression will be the second most common illness on the planet (after infectious disease). Can you believe that? At the rate we're going, I can see this to be true. My hope is that you take my message to heart and begin to turn things around. You may feel like freeing yourself from the clutches of debt and despair is next to impossible, but I'm here to tell you it's not. Take little steps. One day at a time.

When you pay attention to what matters in life, you'll find that those things don't cost very much monetarily. They require time, effort, and energy but often can't be bought. I'm talking about relationships, independence, health, career, self-reliance, and family. These are among the things that bring you joy and fill your life with meaning, laughter, and personal satisfaction. The more you do spend, though, and clutter your life with debt and cramped quarters, the less time and energy you will have to devote to these important things. Sure, you'll have more stuff but you'll also have less joy, less stability, less control of your life, and huge emotional voids.

It should come as no surprise, then, that of all the questions I've asked you in this book, the most important one to ask yourself today and every day is this: **Where do I derive happiness?** Strip away the things that steal your happiness. Embrace the fact that less is more. You can have everything you need to be healthy, happy, and lead a productive life if you just peel away the nonessentials that distract you and drag you—and your time, energy, and of course finances—down. Learning to live within your means will not happen overnight, nor will it be "easy." But from that very first moment you sense a small lift from living with less stuff, less debt, and less stress, you will instantly have more motivation to continue peeling more and more layers away. And the more you empty out the junk that keeps you away from your vision, the closer you'll get to realizing that vision. The more room you'll have to fill it with what you value and cherish most.

What I love about my job is that I wholeheartedly believe an organized life provides the foundation for whatever you want to accomplish. Decluttering the physical spaces around you can serve as an entry point to making the kinds of dramatic changes in your life that you dream of achieving, but which haven't happened in the past despite a great many good intentions and sheer force of willpower. Let's face it: diets don't work; New Year's resolutions fade within weeks; and reprogramming your mind and body that are used to a certain lifestyle is a mighty tall order.

The most effective way to move forward is to choose just one thing—*one thing*—to change and then let that one thing be your launch pad for further change. You may choose to work backward in this book and start with your physical surroundings. Let that be your one thing to get going if dealing with your personal life is too hard right away. After all, your physical surroundings are concrete and right before your very eyes. Tackling them is relatively easy using the initial steps I've outlined in this book regarding your stuff. You'll find that this single action will spill into your having to then face your debt, your personal issues with loved ones, and your relationship with yourself. Don't be fooled by this last encounter, for I often find that the overwhelming tension and stress people experience in their lives—that crushing out-of-control feeling—and which manifests itself in their cluttered worlds and troubled relationships, is deeply rooted in the unhealthy, disconnected relationship they have with themselves. You could be your own worst enemy. And the silver lining in that truth is that you are your own best solution. Start small. Start simply. Start with yourself in just a single room and watch what happens. Then enlist others to help champion your goals and the vision you have for your life. The exercises I've outlined in this book will guide you through it all, each one building on the other and culminating in results that will move you forward.

Make today the beginning of a new path. Remember, take it one step at a time. I trust you'll be surprised by what you can do. Your limitations will expand. Your passion for life will grow. Your belief that less really is more will become abundantly clear. Your happiness will root itself firmly. And the possibilities in your future will proliferate alongside your prosperity.

Now get to it!

acknowledgments

RARE IS THE PERSON who has not been slammed—and slammed hard—by the recent economic meltdown. We see its effects every time we turn on the TV, read a newspaper, or gather to chat with friends. Everyone has been touched. Regardless of the economic meltdown—or maybe because of it—I continue to be inundated daily with requests for help to deal with homes overflowing with clutter, to assist families whose stuff has taken over, and to help people get back on track from a life derailed by the sheer volume of clutter they're drowning in.

Having written about physical and emotional clutter, and explored the relationship between clutter and weight, it seemed natural to examine how our obsession with more stuff has contributed to our current financial mess and sense of deep unhappiness with what we have and where we are. Happiness is the most elusive of gifts. Chase it and it escapes you. Attempt to buy it, and you'll almost certainly be disappointed. Happiness, in my experience, never comes with more stuff—a lesson I see people learning the hard way almost every day.

One of our inalienable rights is the pursuit of happiness. Discovering and enjoying it is another matter altogether. A common refrain I hear when helping people deal with their clutter is "But I thought all this stuff would make me happy." I have a particular take on all this, hence what you're currently holding in your hands. It's an attempt to connect some of the dots between what we have, what we want, and the lives we live.

No book writes itself and I, for one, could never do it without the help and support of a great number of people:

To Ken—who continues to be the quiet force behind any success I might achieve.

To my family—near and far—whose support, love, and enthusiasm are unwavering.

To Lydia Wills—a great agent, an excellent advisor and a good friend.

To my colleagues and friends at Simon & Schuster/Free Press: Suzanne Donahue and Carisa Hays especially. An amazing team of professionals whose support and encouragement is enthusiastically given and gratefully received.

To the teams at Harpo in Chicago and the Oprah Winfrey Network (OWN) in Los Angeles. It's been a great trip working with everyone from *The Oprah Winfrey Show,* Oprah Radio, OWN, and Oprah.com. Their friendship, encouragement, and support have been invaluable—thanks to some of the most talented people in the business.

To Kristin Loberg—my collaborator and a remarkable wordsmith. Her gift with the written word is truly amazing and I am so grateful to have her on my team. This book owes much to her.

Last, but definitely not least, there is you—the reader. Without your constant support, unbridled enthusiasm, endless emails and insightful feedback I could never do what I do. Many of you will recognize yourself in these pages because without you this book would not have been possible. I am constantly humbled by the generosity of people to share their stories, their insights, and their lives with me. I have received thousands of emails and each tells a tale that has affected the words on these pages.

From my heart—thank you all!

Described by *The New York Times* as "a genius," Peter Walsh is a clutter expert and organizational consultant who characterizes himself as part contractor and part therapist. He is a regular guest on *The Oprah Winfrey Show* and is the featured organizer on the hit TLC show *Clean Sweep* and hosts *Enough Already! with Peter Walsh* on The Oprah Winfrey Network (OWN). Peter holds a master's degree with a specialty in educational psychology. He divides his time between Los Angeles and Melbourne, Australia.